IAN HALLARD

Ian Hallard is an actor and writer.

His acting credits include *The Boys in the Band* (Park/Vaudeville Theatres), for which he was nominated as Best Actor in the 2017 Whatsonstage Awards, *Hogarth's Progress* (Rose Theatre, Kingston), *Lovesong of the Electric Bear* (Hope/Arts Theatre), *Scenes from an Execution* and *Great Britain* (National Theatre). TV and film roles include *Doctor Who*, *Poirot*, *Endeavour*, *The Crown*, *Sherlock* and *Mary, Queen of Scots*.

Writing includes three episodes of *Poirot* for ITV.

After over twenty years as a performer, he started writing for the stage mere months before a global pandemic closed down all the theatres and left everybody wondering if they would ever reopen. He took this very personally.

As a result, *Adventurous*, which he both wrote and appeared in, was produced online by Jermyn Street Theatre in March 2021. Other writing for theatre includes *Steenie*, about the relationship between James I and the Duke of Buckingham, which was performed at the Turbine Theatre as part of their *Rally Fest* of LGBT+ writing, and *Horse-Play* at Riverside Studios.

Other Titles in this Series

Mike Bartlett
THE 47TH
ALBION
BULL
GAME
AN INTERVENTION
KING CHARLES III
MIKE BARTLETT PLAYS: TWO
MRS DELGADO
SCANDALTOWN
SNOWFLAKE
VASSA *after* Gorky
WILD

Chris Bush
THE ASSASSINATION OF KATIE HOPKINS
THE CHANGING ROOM
FAUSTUS: THAT DAMNED WOMAN
HUNGRY
JANE EYRE *after* Brontë
THE LAST NOËL
ROCK PAPER SCISSORS
STANDING AT THE SKY'S EDGE
    with Richard Hawley
STEEL

Jez Butterworth
THE FERRYMAN
JERUSALEM
JEZ BUTTERWORTH PLAYS: ONE
JEZ BUTTERWORTH PLAYS: TWO
MOJO
THE NIGHT HERON
PARLOUR SONG
THE RIVER
THE WINTERLING

Caryl Churchill
BLUE HEART
CHURCHILL PLAYS: THREE
CHURCHILL PLAYS: FOUR
CHURCHILL PLAYS: FIVE
CHURCHILL: SHORTS
CLOUD NINE
DING DONG THE WICKED
A DREAM PLAY *after* Strindberg
DRUNK ENOUGH TO SAY I LOVE YOU?
ESCAPED ALONE
FAR AWAY
GLASS. KILL. BLUEBEARD'S FRIENDS.
    IMP.
HERE WE GO
HOTEL
ICECREAM
LIGHT SHINING IN BUCKINGHAMSHIRE
LOVE AND INFORMATION
MAD FOREST
A NUMBER
PIGS AND DOGS
SEVEN JEWISH CHILDREN
THE SKRIKER
THIS IS A CHAIR
THYESTES *after* Seneca
TRAPS
WHAT IF IF ONLY

Natasha Gordon
NINE NIGHT

Stephen Karam
THE HUMANS
SONS OF THE PROPHET
SPEECH & DEBATE

Lucy Kirkwood
BEAUTY AND THE BEAST
    with Katie Mitchell
BLOODY WIMMIN
THE CHILDREN
CHIMERICA
HEDDA *after* Ibsen
IT FELT EMPTY WHEN THE HEART
    WENT AT FIRST BUT IT IS
    ALRIGHT NOW
LUCY KIRKWOOD PLAYS: ONE
MOSQUITOES
NSFW
RAPTURE
TINDERBOX
THE WELKIN

Rob Madge
MY SON'S A QUEER
    (BUT WHAT CAN YOU DO?)

Suzie Miller
PRIMA FACIE

Lauryn Redding
BLOODY ELLE

Jack Thorne
2ND MAY 1997
AFTER LIFE
BUNNY
BURYING YOUR BROTHER IN
    THE PAVEMENT
A CHRISTMAS CAROL *after* Dickens
THE END OF HISTORY...
HOPE
JACK THORNE PLAYS: ONE
JUNKYARD
LET THE RIGHT ONE IN
    after John Ajvide Lindqvist
MYDIDAE
THE SOLID LIFE OF SUGAR WATER
STACY & FANNY AND FAGGOT
WHEN YOU CURE ME
WOYZECK *after* Büchner

debbie tucker green
BORN BAD
DEBBIE TUCKER GREEN PLAYS: ONE
DIRTY BUTTERFLY
EAR FOR EYE
HANG
NUT
A PROFOUNDLY AFFECTIONATE,
    PASSIONATE DEVOTION TO
    SOMEONE (– *NOUN*)
RANDOM
STONING MARY
TRADE & GENERATIONS
TRUTH AND RECONCILIATION

Phoebe Waller-Bridge
FLEABAG

Amanda Whittington
BE MY BABY
KISS ME QUICKSTEP
LADIES' DAY
LADIES DOWN UNDER
LADIES UNLEASHED
MIGHTY ATOMS
SATIN 'N' STEEL
THE THRILL OF LOVE

Ian Hallard

THE WAY OLD FRIENDS DO

NICK HERN BOOKS
London
www.nickhernbooks.co.uk

A Nick Hern Book

The Way Old Friends Do first published in Great Britain as a paperback original in 2023 by Nick Hern Books Limited, The Glasshouse, 49a Goldhawk Road, London W12 8QP

The Way Old Friends Do copyright © 2023 Ian Hallard

Ian Hallard has asserted his right to be identified as the author of this work

Lyrics to 'Way Old Friends Do, The' written by Benny Goran Bror Andersson, Bjoern K. Ulvaeus and used by kind permission of Universal Music Publishing Ltd. on behalf of Universal/Union Songs Musikforlag AB

Cover design by Steph Pyne

Designed and typeset by Nick Hern Books, London

Printed in Great Britain by Mimeo Ltd, Huntingdon, Cambridgeshire PE29 6XX

A CIP catalogue record for this book is available from the British Library

ISBN 978 1 83904 119 8

Introduction
Ian Hallard

Saturday 6th April 1974 was a pretty special day for me. That spring evening saw a sequin-strewn Swedish quartet make their debut on the international stage, as they swept to victory at the Eurovision Song Contest with their glam-rock inspired banger 'Waterloo'. I don't have any specific memories of that night. Indeed, it would be rather strange if I had, as I hadn't yet been born. My mother, however, tuned in, as she did every year, and as she was a couple of months pregnant with me at the time, who knows? Maybe some kind of musical osmosis occurred...

Whatever the source of my obsession, ABBA have been the soundtrack to my life: no doubt about it! As a child, I would dance around our living room to ABBA LPs, pretending to be Agnetha, in a pair of yellow woollen plaits my mum had made for me. My teenage years coincided with the dark period in the eighties when ABBA became so deeply unfashionable, only the bravest or most foolhardy admitted to enjoying their music. And now, here we are in the present day, their genius finally acknowledged, with their popularity maybe even greater than it was in their 1970s heyday.

Why do I adore them so? It's hard to quantify precisely. It's Benny's infuriatingly catchy melodies, beautifully arranged with an apparent simplicity that belies the intricacy that lies beneath them. It's Frida's honey-smooth, mellifluous mezzo voice, and the way it both complements and contrasts with Agnetha's piercing pop soprano. And it's all tied together by business mastermind Björn's acumen and, increasingly, as the years progressed, astute lyrics. Their success in some ways could not be more mainstream, and yet they've always held a special place in the hearts of LGBTQ+ people. Which is ironic given that their initial image could not have been more heterosexual. Are they camp? Undoubtedly so at times. It's there in the two women's knowing winks and eyelash fluttering in the video for 'Take a Chance On Me', in Frida's *Cabaret*-style delivery of 'Money, Money, Money', and in Agnetha's devastating performance in 'The Winner Takes It All': all dishevelled perm and abundant blue eyeshadow. But that's not to say that they shouldn't be taken seriously. After all, my ultra-macho, karate black-belt wielding Uncle Mick was reduced to weeping when he heard 'Slipping Through My Fingers' for the first time. Anyway, it's pointless trying to analyse why they touch my soul in the way they do. They just do.

In the summer of 2019, I sat down to try and write my first play. They say to write what you know, and so I thought, well, why not write about ABBA? Extensive googling confirmed to me that nearly thirty years since Björn Again had first tottered on stage in their platform boots, nobody had ever thought of putting a cross-dressing twist on an ABBA tribute band, and that was that. I was off! Admittedly, I did have to clarify to a selection of excited friends who, when I told them what I was doing, mistakenly thought that I was actually setting up a drag ABBA tribute band, rather than just writing a play about one.

I wanted to write a role for myself, and so the character of Peter – a Brummie on the 'rainbow spectrum' and a devotee of ABBA – was born. He's certainly not a million miles away from the real-life me, although I should add that none of the major events in the play are autobiographical. For better or worse, I have never become romantically entangled with a gorgeous but Machiavellian Australian photographer. Having said that, one Saturday afternoon in June 2016, when I first watched the footage of Frida and Agnetha's unexpected onstage reunion at Berns restaurant in Stockholm, my husband came in from walking the dog to find me sobbing at my laptop, and was genuinely alarmed that something terrible had happened. Oh, and I did cry when my parents took me to see *ABBA: The Movie* because I didn't want it to end. And the first time I watched *ABBA: A Video Documentary*, when it got to 1982 and they split up, I cried then as well. So, basically all the crying bits are absolutely inspired by real-life events.

Once I'd had the initial idea, I wrote like a demon and got a first draft down within a week. How did that differ from the text you have in your hands, you may wonder? Well, the eccentric, glossary-loving, Palin-skeptic Mrs Campbell sadly did not feature in that initial version, whereas an extended flashback sequence which dramatised Edward and Peter's schooldays did. (I quickly realised this was just backstory and did not need to be included. Plus, the sight of two forty-something actors playing thirteen-year-olds threatened to take the play dangerously into *Blood Brothers* territory...)

I liked the idea that the audience never see the band performing, so it's left to one's imagination how good (or bad) the act actually is. I also knew that the structure of the play had to lead up to a final scene where Peter and Edward sing the title song to each other; and that the final scene would take place on the night when ABBA's new recordings were finally revealed to the world. It's strange to think that when I wrote the play's final line – 'I Still Have Faith in You' – I had no idea what that song would sound like or when that night might be.

The Way Old Friends Do is about friendship, love, obsession; being queer, being middle-aged, being a fan. In short, it's about devotion, desire and 'Dancing Queens'. Elements of the dynamic between the characters of Edward and Peter are based on my relationship with my dear friend and sometime colleague, Matthew Baldwin. I am indebted to him for his ongoing generosity, kindness and inspiration. This play simply wouldn't have happened without him.

As I write this, we're in the midst of rehearsals for the show's first production. I'm delighted and honoured to be working with a company of supremely talented comic actors who are bringing my play to life. If our audiences experience even a fraction of the fun and laughter we're having in the rehearsal room, then they're in for a good time. It feels scary to be putting something out there that is so uniquely personal to me. I can only hope that audiences will enjoy it, and that, in these somewhat scary and uncertain times, it will put a smile on people's faces. And for you, reading the play, I hope you enjoy it too. You don't have to be an ABBA fan to enjoy it, but I think it will help!

Who'd have thought that, forty-five years on, that little boy in the woollen yellow plaits, dancing around his living room to 'Take a Chance On Me', would grow up to do pretty much the same thing, but this time, professionally and on the stage at the Birmingham Repertory Theatre? It's a crazy world…

Acknowledgements

So many people have helped and supported me in getting *The Way Old Friends Do* from page to stage. I'm sure I'll have forgotten some, so my sincere apologies if I have missed anyone.

To the actors who have performed in rehearsed readings over the years: Kitty Archer, Matthew Baldwin, Ruby Bentall, Timothy Blore, Doña Croll, Peter Forbes, Michelle Gayle, Katherine Jakeways, Joseph Timms and Francesca Wilding.

And to those who performed in the show's original production: Donna Berlin, James Bradshaw, Sara Crowe, Toby Holloway, Andrew Horton, Tariyé Peterside, Rose Shalloo and Anton Tweedale, along with national treasures Miriam Margolyes and Paul O'Grady who so kindly recorded voice-overs for the show. (Although, weirdly, and just between us, neither Miriam nor Paul actually like ABBA!)

To the creative team: Janet Bird, Andrew Exeter, Ben Harrison, Marc Frankum and Gavin Joseph; our stage managers Megan Bly and James Prendergast; and indeed all the numerous behind-the-scenes folk: freelancers, staff at the Birmingham Rep and Seabright Productions, and all the touring venues for the show's premiere.

To Caroline Chignell at PBJ Management and Nick Errington and everyone at Grantham Hazeldine; Paul Sullivan and Reetu Kabra; Matt Applewhite and Sarah Liisa Wilkinson at Nick Hern Books; and a special thanks to Görel Hanser and the licensing team at Universal for all their help.

To numerous people for having such confidence in the play: among them, Sean Foley at the Birmingham Rep; James Seabright, Tom O'Connell and Jason Haigh-Ellery; Jez Bond at Park Theatre, who contacted Benny in Stockholm and secured not only ABBA's blessing for the show to go ahead, but precious permission to sing the title song; and to Mark for his love and encouragement. I can think of nobody else who I could better trust to direct my 'baby'.

And finally to Anni-Frid, Benny, Björn and Agnetha. Thank you for everything. Without a song or a dance, what are we?

I.H.

A Note for Amateur Companies

The business of music licensing is complex, so I knew when I wrote the very first draft of this play, that there was no guarantee we'd get permission to perform any ABBA songs in the show. That's at least part of the reason why the play's focus remains very much on the backstage events in the turbulent career of Head Over Heels.

If you are mounting your own production, fortunately, a venue's PRS licence should cover you for permission for all the music that connects one scene to the next, and your production will therefore be able to include some ABBA songs. As long as the track is transitional or in the background, and the characters neither perform, refer to, or interact with the song in question, no specific additional licence is required.

There are two exceptions to this in the play. The first occurs in Act One, Scene Six, when Edward performs his dance solo. We used specially composed music for this moment, and did not seek to license the live recording of 'Gimme! Gimme! Gimme!'

The second occasion is when Peter and Edward sing the title song to one another in Act Two, Scene Nine. We were fortunate that the lovely people at Universal Music granted permission for us to perform one verse of 'The Way Old Friends Do'. There's nothing to stop you seeking similar permission, although bear in mind there will be a licensing fee to pay.

However, if you are not able to include the song, the following dialogue can be substituted in its place:

EDWARD. So, this evening. What made you get in touch? After all this time?

PETER. You know how the song goes, Edward.

EDWARD. Which song?

PETER. 'The Way Old Friends Do'.

He pauses. He looks at EDWARD *hopefully. He takes a deep breath and starts to sing.*

'You – '

EDWARD. No! Please. I beg of you. Don't sing. I can't bear it. It's too cheesy.

PETER. Okay. Then answer me this. Can we face it together?

EDWARD. Yes. Of course we can.

PETER *smiles.*

It hasn't ruined it for you then? What happened with Head Over Heels. You still listen to the music?

The Way Old Friends Do was first performed at the
Birmingham Rep Studio Theatre on 17 February 2023, before
touring to Sheffield Theatres; Park Theatre, London; Yvonne
Arnaud Theatre, Guildford; Northcott Theatre, Exeter; Theatre
Royal Brighton; Everyman Theatre, Cheltenham; Oxford
Playhouse; The Lowry, Salford; Theatre Royal Bath and York
Theatre Royal. The cast and creative team was as follows:

JODIE	Rose Shalloo
SALLY	Donna Berlin
PETER	Ian Hallard
NAN	Miriam Margolyes
EDWARD	James Bradshaw
WAITER	Andrew Horton
MRS CAMPBELL	Sara Crowe
CHRISTIAN	Andrew Horton
RADIO HOST	Paul O'Grady

UNDERSTUDIES
WAITER/CHRISTIAN/ASM	Toby Holloway
JODIE/SALLY/MRS CAMPBELL	Tariyé Peterside
PETER/EDWARD	Anton Tweedale

Director	Mark Gatiss
Set and Costume Designer	Janet Bird
Lighting Designer	Andrew Exeter
Sound Designer	Ben Harrison
Casting Director	Mark Frankum CDG
Producers	Birmingham Rep
	& James Seabright
	in association with
	Jason Haigh-Ellery
	and Park Theatre

14

PRODUCTION TEAM

Assistant Director	Gavin Joseph
Costume Supervisor	Kay Wilton
Props Supervisor	Claire Browne
Production Managers	Ian Taylor
	& James Anderton
Company Stage Manager on Book	Megan Bly
Assistant Stage Manager	James Prendergast
Head of Wardrobe & Wigs	Emily Leaff Pond
Production Relighter & Electrician	Joe Samuels
Production Carpenter	Thomas Baum
Lighting Programmer	Oliver Colley

BIRMINGHAM REP PRODUCTION CREDITS

Executive Director	Rachael Thomas
Artistic Director	Sean Foley
Senior Producer	Jonathan Brindley

SEABRIGHT PRODUCTIONS

Producer	James Seabright
Co-Producer	Tom O'Connell
Associate Producer	Jack Robertson
Marketing Director	Kate Farrell
Head of Production	Luke Gledsdale
Stage One Trainee Producer	Magdalene Dorling
Bookkeeper	Alan Mackintosh

THE WAY OLD FRIENDS DO PRODUCTION CREDITS

Publicity Design	Steph Pyne
Production Photography	Darren Bell
Press Representative	Paul Sullivan
Social Media Manager	Mark Ludmon
Set Built by	The Rep Workshop Team
Scenic Painting by	The Rep Paintshop Team
Lighting Prepped and Practicals made by	The Rep Lighting Team
Sound Prepped by	The Rep Sound Team
Costumes made and sourced by	The Rep Wardrobe Team

With thanks to all Rep Staff and Volunteers who have worked on this production.

For Mum
Thank you for the music –
for giving it to me

Characters

JODIE, *twenties*
SALLY, *forties*
PETER, *forties*
EDWARD, *forties*
WAITER, *twenties*
MRS CAMPBELL, *sixties*
CHRISTIAN, *twenties*
NAN, *eighties, voice-over*
RADIO DJ, *voice-over*

Time Settings

April 2015 – August 2016.

September 2021.

This text went to press before the end of rehearsals and so may differ slightly from the play as performed.

Pre-set

RADIO DJ (*voice-over*). Eight years. [*'Eight years' should be amended to however long has actually passed since 2015*.] A lot can happen in that time, can't it?

I mean, eight years ago, nobody had heard of lockdowns, of 'Take Back Control', or *The Masked Singer*. And the idea of Donald Trump becoming President of the United States… well that seemed as ridiculous as Boris Johnson becoming Prime Minister here.

So, why don't you make sure your phone's switched off, sit back and relax as we take you to a theatre dressing room, somewhere in the West Midlands, back in the simpler time that was the spring of 2015?

ACT ONE

Scene One: Dressing Room

June 2015.

Darkness.

A female voice is in the middle of an a cappella vocal warm-up. She attempts some arpeggios and does a little sirening. She has an adequate voice but it's clear she is not going to be challenging Adele any time soon.

The lights fade up on a small, tatty dressing room. The voice belongs to JODIE *(twenties). She has her eyes closed. She also has earphones in, and is singing along to a track on her phone.*

A woman in her forties, SALLY, *carrying a couple of Tesco bags, enters quietly.* SALLY *stands watching* JODIE *for a moment.*

The vocal warm-up continues. Eventually, JODIE *takes a deep breath and launches into some lyrics:*

JODIE. 'The winner takes…'

Her top note is flat and she knows it. She opens her eyes and rips the earphones out.

Bollocks!

SALLY *smiles at* JODIE. JODIE *is a little taken aback.*

Oh God, I'm sorry. I didn't hear you come in. I had my earphones – You see, I'm a bit jittery. And I struggle with the octave leap when I get nervous.

SALLY *rolls her eyes sympathetically.*

It's actually kind of authentic. Agnetha – (*Pronounces it Agg-nee-thuh.*) struggled to sing in tune apparently. They had to re-record her vocals in the studio. I did some research.

SALLY *opens her mouth to speak but before she can –*

I don't suppose you know how many people they're seeing, do you? I mean, the money's not great, and they were a bit vague on the phone. Are they looking to cast the whole group, do you know? And there was a typo in the advert too. I did think: am I wasting my time here? But they said they needed someone ASAP and that would really suit me because I have to move out at the end of this month. The girl I'm subletting my room from is coming back from Brazil earlier than she expected. She thinks she's being set up as a drug donkey. Do I mean donkey? Sorry. Mule. Drug mule. So this would really help me out. Things have been so quiet. I've given up on ever hearing from my agent again. And I worked as an au pair in Stockholm in my gap year, which always makes everyone laugh, because the au pair is usually Swedish, not the other way round. But basically it means I can do the accent pretty well. So I thought that would help too. And – Oh, I'm sorry. I'm babbling. I do that when I get nervous. I forgot to bring my Rescue Remedy.

A beat.

You probably don't have a clue what I'm talking about. I'm auditioning, you see. There was an advert in *The Stage* newspaper for an ABBA tribute band. I know, right? Just what the world needs. *Another* ABBA tribute band! And they hadn't even proofread it properly! They said they were looking for female singers to join the group to play Björn and Benny. And I double-checked – and of course, those are the men! So I thought – well, that's obviously a mistake, but when I rang the number, I didn't say anything. When I was at drama school, I corrected a director who thought an Olivier was an actor. I told him it was either a theatre or an award and he really wasn't happy. He only ever cast me as men after that. We had too many girls in our group, you see. My Stanley Kowalski was… not good.

SALLY *watches her.*

Oh I'm so sorry. I assumed – I just assumed you could speak English. I should have asked. I would usually ask. But that's what happens when I get nervous…

SALLY. Two pieces of advice. One: It's pronounced 'Ann-yett-a'. If you say 'Agg-nee-thuh' you'll be out of here before you sing a note. And two: don't be nervous.

Transition: 'The Winner Takes It All' by ABBA.

Scene Two: Peter's Flat

April 2015.

An unopened bottle of wine and two glasses sit expectantly on a table.

PETER (*forty years old, Brummie accent*) *hums along to the CD.*

The phone starts to ring. He grabs the remote control and turns the CD down. Then he crosses to the phone and presses the loudspeaker button.

PETER. Hi, Nan. You okay?

We hear NAN*'s voice* (*eighties, also Brummie*).

NAN (*voice-over*). How did you know it was me?

PETER. You're the only person I know who still uses the landline. It was either you or someone asking if I'd been mis-sold PPI.

NAN (*voice-over*). Oh, right.

PETER. How are you doing?

PETER *continues to bustle around the flat. He puts wax in his hair and starts to style it.*

NAN (*voice-over*). My bunion's not great but I mustn't grumble. I was just wondering if you're still coming for lunch next weekend.

PETER. Yeah – I should be. Can I confirm for definite in the week?

NAN (*voice-over*). I just need to know if I'm defrosting the pork chops. You waiting to see if you get a better offer?

PETER (*laughing unconvincingly*). No! Of course not. I might have a meeting about a job that's all.

NAN (*voice-over*). On a Sunday?

PETER. Yeah. I know it's... unusual.

NAN (*voice-over*). Oh that's good though! Who's it with?

PETER. Erm... I'd rather not say. Don't want to jinx it, you know.

NAN (*voice-over*). You do like your little secrets! You were always the same. Even as a little boy. That's the Scorpio in you, that is.

PETER. You know that's bollocks, don't you, Nan?

NAN (*voice-over*). Peter! Don't say that. I don't like to hear you swear.

PETER. Bollocks isn't swearing, is it?

NAN (*voice-over*). What is it then?

The doorbell rings.

PETER. Listen, can I call you tomorrow? I've got company.

NAN (*voice-over*). Oh! Anyone I know?

PETER. Don't think so.

NAN (*voice-over*). You see. Scorpio!

PETER. I've got to go. Love you.

NAN (*voice-over*). Love you too, darling. Hope to see you next Sunday.

She hangs up. PETER *has a final 'spritz' of aftershave, glances around to check the flat looks okay, and opens the door.*

PETER *stands there open-mouthed.*

A long beat.

EDWARD (*offstage*). Bugger. Bugger. Me.

PETER *half-groans, half-laughs, as he backs into the room.*

PETER. What are the odds – ?

EDWARD (*offstage*). This is utterly ridiculous. I don't – I mean – oh, *bollocks*.

PETER. Are you just going to stand there swearing?

EDWARD. Bollocks isn't swearing.

PETER. That's what *I* said!

EDWARD. What?

PETER. Oh, it doesn't matter. Are you going to come in?

EDWARD (*offstage*). I don't know. Am I?

PETER. Well, can you shut the door while you're making up your mind? There's a hell of a draught.

EDWARD (*forty, RP accent*) *enters. They stand looking at each other.*

EDWARD. I knew it. I *bloody* knew it. All the – (*Adopting a Brummie accent.*) 'Oh I don't mind what you are. I'm totally cool with it. Look at how cool and tolerant I am.' What was I thinking? No man on this planet as obsessed with ABBA as you were could possibly be straight.

PETER. Have you finished?

EDWARD. This is just typical, this is. This is bloody typical. I have no luck.

PETER. What are you talking about?

EDWARD. Oh, never mind.

PETER. Do you want a drink?

EDWARD. Of course I want a bloody drink. I had to get through a bottle of Rioja just to build up the courage to come here.

PETER. A *bottle*?!

EDWARD. Don't panic. I got a cab. You always were a goody two-shoes.

PETER *opens the wine bottle.*

PETER. Do you want to take your coat off? Sit down?

EDWARD. This is *not* going to happen by the way.

PETER. Yeah. I think that's something we can both agree on.

EDWARD *takes off his coat but doesn't sit.* PETER *pours the wine and brings a glass to* EDWARD. *He chinks his glass.*

Cheers!

EDWARD *glares at him.*

I don't understand why you're so annoyed. It's actually kind of funny if you think about it.

EDWARD *drinks silently.*

Look: if you'd sent a face pic like I asked, this would never have happened.

EDWARD. Well, you didn't send me one.

PETER. Didn't see why I should if you weren't going to.

EDWARD. I mean I *did* send you a picture of my –

PETER. Well I was hardly likely to recognise you from that, was I?

EDWARD. I suppose not.

A beat.

PETER. I mean, it's a perfectly nice –

EDWARD. Perhaps we could draw a discreet veil over that particular part of my anatomy?

PETER. Sure. Fine by me.

EDWARD. This is why people hate Grindr. I see that now. It's all fucking about and no actual fucking.

PETER. Once in a while something pays off, though, no?

EDWARD. I wouldn't know.

PETER. What do you mean?

EDWARD. I've never even done it before. First time I actually pluck up the courage to use the bloody thing – and I end up connecting with you of all people.

PETER. Yeah, I suppose that is a bit unlucky. I'm surprised you didn't get snapped up straight away though. Fresh meat. In every sense.

EDWARD. I made the mistake of putting my actual age.

PETER. Excuse me? You're not thirty-four. You're three months younger than me.

EDWARD. Fuck you.

PETER. You've not taken your wedding ring off either. Did you just forget or is it a statement?

EDWARD. Fuck you again.

PETER. Look, why don't we view this as fate? A chance to catch up? How long's it been? Twenty-one, twenty-two years? Or should I knock six years off that as well?

EDWARD (*sarcastically*). Ha ha. Listen, if I'd wanted a reunion, I'd have looked you up on Facebook.

PETER. I'm not on Facebook. Don't trust it. Look, Eddie, surely you can see the funny side of this?

EDWARD. Nobody calls me Eddie. You didn't do it at school. Don't start now.

PETER. Sorry. Why don't you sit down? Let's forget about Grindr and get pissed. (*He holds up the bottle of wine.*) I've got plenty more where this came from.

EDWARD *relents a little and sits.*

EDWARD. Oh, all right then.

PETER. So, fill me in.

EDWARD makes a suggestive noise and gives him a pointed look.

I forgot you do that. You're married then?

EDWARD (*still reluctant*). Hmm.

He finally gives in.

Well, civil partnership. We haven't got round to it yet but we are planning on putting in for the upgrade.

PETER. You make it sound like air miles! What's his name?

EDWARD. Melvyn.

PETER. Melvyn? That's – nice.

EDWARD. No it isn't. It's bloody awful. I'd really like to call him something else. Sometimes I do.

PETER. What does he do?

EDWARD. He's retired. He used to work in the City. He's – a fair bit older than me.

PETER. Oh. Sugar daddy, eh? How did you meet?

EDWARD. I'd forgotten what an inquisitive little sod you are. If you really must know, he was a friend of my father's.

PETER. Ooh… I imagine that went down well.

EDWARD. Things are a bit more straightforward now Father is no longer with us. Mother is still doing her best ostrich impression.

PETER. Is she still in the same house?

EDWARD. Yes, I'm paying the obligatory filial visit.

PETER. So I guess Melvyn isn't with you?

EDWARD. Ha! Ostrich – remember.

PETER. How long have you two been together?

EDWARD. Oh, from the moment I emerged howling and screaming from her vagina!

A look from PETER.

Sorry. Do you remember I used to get facetious when I felt anxious? Well, that hasn't changed. If you must know, Melvyn and I will celebrate our nineteenth anniversary this October.

PETER. Congratulations! God, what's that in gay years?

EDWARD. Four hundred.

PETER. Right. Have you eaten by the way? Do you want anything?

EDWARD. No. It'll soak up the booze.

PETER. I'll get us some Pringles.

PETER *exits to the kitchen and returns with a bowl.*

Here you go.

EDWARD. Thanks.

PETER. Are you really feeling anxious?

EDWARD. Constantly. (*Raising his wine glass.*) This is helping though.

PETER. I'm sorry we lost touch.

EDWARD. It happens, doesn't it? We were school friends, that's all. We didn't make a pact for life. It was hardly *Blood Brothers*.

PETER. Good job really. The common kid ends up shooting the posh one.

EDWARD. I've never seen it. Scouse accents bring me out in a rash.

PETER. Still. I could have made an effort.

EDWARD. We were kids. I went off to uni. You stayed put. And of course, things were never really the same after we did that concert.

PETER. Funny, isn't it? How shame lingers. I can remember how I felt that afternoon like it was yesterday.

EDWARD. Anyway, it's all changed now. No shame in being an ABBA fan any more. Everybody loves them. You were ahead of your time.

PETER. Nice to be proved right in the end.

EDWARD. I still don't think it went that badly.

PETER. That's because you were anaesthetised by your crush on Jonathan Harris. He asked you to do it – and you couldn't say no.

EDWARD *has finished his wine. He offers his empty glass to* PETER, *who refills it.*

EDWARD. He was lovely. Always thought he had a look of Chesney Hawkes. I told you all my schoolboy crushes. You never said a word. Didn't you trust me?

PETER. It wasn't like that. I didn't know myself. I thought I was completely straight.

EDWARD. Ha!

PETER. Bisexuality is a thing, you know. I went out with Liz Frost after we left school.

EDWARD. Listen, darling. I had a falafel wrap for lunch. Doesn't make me a fucking vegetarian.

PETER. Liz and I dated for three months.

EDWARD. A whole three months? Gosh! And?

PETER. And what?

EDWARD. How was it?

PETER. Not great, to be honest. Liz was the first person I ever kissed. And every time we snogged, I'd end up with this huge, wet patch down my shirt. I got so paranoid that it was me. So I used to suck and swallow the spit to stop it happening. It was only after we split up that I realised it was her, not me. It was such a relief. Although I had spent three months hoovering up Elizabeth Frost's saliva.

EDWARD. That's revolting. Wasn't that enough to put you off women for life?

PETER. No. I've had some very lovely experiences over the years.

EDWARD. If you say so. Anything serious?

PETER. Yeah, a couple were pretty long term, but certainly nothing to compare to you and Melvyn.

EDWARD. And you're single now?

PETER. Yep. Welcome to my Balsall Common bachelor pad!

EDWARD. What did your nan say when – ? Oh, is she still with us?

PETER. Yes. I mean, she's getting on a bit now…

EDWARD. How did she take the news?

PETER. What news?

EDWARD. Your 'bisexuality'.

PETER. She doesn't know.

EDWARD. What?

PETER. If I met a bloke and it got serious, it would be different. There'd be something concrete to tell her. As it is – well, I don't really think an eighty-four-year-old needs to know that I spend my Saturday evenings trawling Grindr.

EDWARD. Only Saturdays? How very restrained.

PETER. And are you happy? With Melvyn?

EDWARD. That's a pretty existential question. We've had our ups and downs, but I don't think we could do without each other.

PETER. That's nice. So…?

An unspoken question hangs there.

EDWARD. So if everything's hunky-dory, why have I gone on Grindr?

PETER. Are you in an open relationship? Lots of guys are nowadays.

EDWARD. And that's your business because…?

PETER. Sorry. I just thought –

EDWARD. Yes, well. My romantic escapades have always been an open book to you. Apparently, you've been a little more circumspect. Well, two can play at that game.

PETER. Okay, okay. Is this really the first time you've used it? Grindr, I mean. Am I allowed to ask that at least?

EDWARD. You are. And it is. My luck really is that shitty. How long have you been on it?

PETER. Oh, I've been whoring my way through it for years.

PETER *takes out his phone and shows it to* EDWARD.

Of the men in the local vicinity, I think I've had one, two, three, four, five… six, seven, eight… nine, ten. Eleven if you count him.

EDWARD. Why wouldn't you count him?

PETER. We met. I couldn't go through with it. Hair *everywhere*. Even his toenails.

EDWARD. First Elizabeth Frost's saliva. Now hairy toenails. Do you *want* me to vomit over your soft furnishings?

PETER (*still looking at his phone*). Oh, this one's new. He's quite hot.

EDWARD. He looks like Nick Clegg.

PETER. Nick Clegg's hot.

EDWARD. Really? Deputy Prime Minister – about to be fucked at the General Election – Nick Clegg?

PETER. Yeah. I'd happily fuck him – General Election or not.

EDWARD. Actually, I think that *is* Nick Clegg.

PETER. Maybe I should message him just in case.

EDWARD. Just in case it is Nick Clegg? You're a kinky bastard, aren't you?

PETER *laughs*.

PETER. It's good to see you.

EDWARD. It's good to see you too.

A beat.

Look, I should go.

PETER. You don't have to.

EDWARD. Told Mother I wouldn't be late.

PETER. Are you not going to try again?

EDWARD. I think my experiment with Grindr is over. This evening has definitely been a message from the divine.

PETER. I thought you might have lapsed by now.

EDWARD. Catholicism is like herpes. It never really goes away.

PETER. Right. I'm meeting a couple of friends for a pub lunch tomorrow. Fancy joining us before you head off?

EDWARD. Why not? Message me on Grindr, okay?

PETER. Yeah. Or we could be really radical and swap numbers?

A beat.

EDWARD. Alright.

He jots down his number.

I'll leave you to get into the Lib Dem leader's pants. Spare a thought for poor Miriam though, won't you?

PETER. Miriam?

EDWARD. González Durántez.

PETER. Huh?

EDWARD. Mrs Clegg.

Transition: 'He Is Your Brother' by ABBA.

Scene Three: Pub Garden

April 2015.

A WAITER *arranges a couple of tables, laying out cutlery and glasses. Then he retreats to his station.*

After a moment, EDWARD *enters. He catches the* WAITER*'s eye.*

EDWARD. Hello.

WAITER. Hi. Are you eating?

EDWARD. We will be, yes.

WAITER. How many of you?

EDWARD. Four.

WAITER. Feel free to sit where you like.

EDWARD (*under his breath*). I know where I'd *like* to sit.

WAITER. I'm sorry?

EDWARD. Nothing!

WAITER. Can I get you a drink?

EDWARD. Glass of Rioja?

WAITER. Small, medium or large?

EDWARD. Medi– Oh, who am I kidding? Large, please.

WAITER (*smiling*). Coming right up!

The WAITER *exits.* EDWARD *sits at the table and immediately pulls out his phone, presses a couple of buttons and scrolls through the screen.*

EDWARD. Bugger.

He puts his phone away and checks his watch. He scans round the pub. He gets his phone out again and scrolls through it idly.

The WAITER *re-enters with* EDWARD*'s wine.*

WAITER. One large glass of Rioja.

EDWARD. Thanks.

PETER *enters and joins* EDWARD *at the table.*

PETER. Been here long?

EDWARD. No. Just got here. (*He raises his glass.*)

WAITER. Can I get you something, sir?

PETER. Pint of bitter shandy, please.

WAITER. Righto.

The WAITER *exits.* PETER *and* EDWARD *both watch him go.*

EDWARD. It's no use. I already checked.

PETER. Checked what?

EDWARD. Grindr. He's not on it.

PETER. I thought you were abandoning Grindr.

EDWARD. I might keep it for research purposes. Anything happen with the Clegg-a-like last night?

PETER. No. He was just looking for dick pics.

EDWARD. Bastard. I hope he loses his seat.

The WAITER *re-enters with the shandy and some menus.*

Talking of losing one's seat…

WAITER. Here you go. And some menus.

PETER. That's great. Cheers.

WAITER. No problem.

The WAITER *exits.*

SALLY *enters, a bottle of Becks in her hand.*

SALLY. Hiya.

SALLY and PETER *hug.*

PETER. Sal – this is my old school friend, Edward. Edward – this is Sally.

EDWARD. Nice to meet you.

SALLY. Likewise.

EDWARD. And how do you two know each other?

PETER. Through my old job.

SALLY. My partner manages the Library Theatre. The library where Peter works. Well, used to work.

PETER. Local authority cuts. I'm a victim of austerity…

EDWARD. Partner? That's suspiciously ambiguous. Are we talking male or female?

SALLY. We're talking female.

EDWARD. God, you're really ticking the diversity boxes, aren't you? Don't suppose you have a disability too? That would give you the full house!

SALLY. I do actually. Have a disability.

EDWARD. Really? Oh Christ, I'm sorry…

SALLY. Yeah, I have this condition. I'm allergic to posh prats in cravats. Makes me feel nauseous.

An awkward silence. Then SALLY *smiles at him – a tad smug.*

PETER (*breaking the tension*). Where is Diane?

SALLY. She had to go into work. Last-minute emergency. Mike Shelby's gone bust.

PETER. Who?

SALLY. A promoter she uses a lot. They've had to cancel tonight's booking.

PETER. What was the show?

SALLY. Elton John tribute act. Crocodile Mock.

EDWARD. Ha! That's simultaneously terrible and brilliant.

SALLY. Well, that describes most of the stuff that gets put on at the theatre. It's mainly tribute bands, kids' dance shows, amateur dramatics…

PETER. Sally's involved with a few of the am-dram societies.

EDWARD. Oh – you're a *thespian* lesbian?

SALLY (*raising an eyebrow*). I don't perform. I do backstage stuff: stage management, props, that kind of thing. I keep trying to get Peter to join. I've heard him sing. His voice isn't bad – and they're always desperate for men.

EDWARD. As is Peter!

PETER. I don't sing in public any more. Not since… Well not since I was a teenager.

EDWARD. You're never going to forgive me for that, are you?

SALLY. What's this?

PETER. Have you ever stood in front of a hall full of eighteen-year-olds pissing themselves laughing? Well, I have and it's not fun.

EDWARD. We were both in the school choir. I persuaded him to sing some ABBA songs with me at the end-of-term concert. He remains traumatised to this day.

SALLY. Mike Shelby was supposed to be doing an ABBA tribute show for Diane in July. That one sold out pretty much straight away. Then there's Proxy Music in September.

EDWARD. Oh, I like that one!

PETER. Do you know what you want to eat? I'll go and order.

EDWARD. Allow me.

He gives a knowing look.

PETER. You don't change. I thought he wasn't on Grindr?

EDWARD. I'm only going to admire the view. What do you want?

PETER. Roast chicken for me.

EDWARD (*glancing in the direction of the* WAITER). Roast chicken... Mmm that does sound appealing...

SALLY. I'll have the beef.

EDWARD. Curtains?

SALLY. What??

EDWARD. Sorry. Involuntary word association. I'm going! I'm going!

EDWARD *exits with the menus.*

SALLY. Is he always like this?

PETER. He'll relax when he knows you better. He always tries too hard to impress people.

SALLY. Really? This is him trying to *impress* me? What would he be like if he was trying to piss me off?

PETER. I feel a bit guilty to be honest. We were inseparable when we were kids. He'd had a rough time. He'd been expelled from his private school for making a pass at another lad. We kind of 'came out' to each other.

SALLY. I thought you were older when you realised you were –

PETER. Oh, I was. No, I mean – Well, he came out to me as gay. I came out as an ABBA fan. I hadn't told anyone before. Only my nan knew. I'm not sure which of us was more mortified.

SALLY. So it never went beyond friendship?

PETER. No, never.

SALLY. And what about now?

PETER. God, no. He's married and I'm – not interested in him that way.

SALLY. You're happy as you are.

PETER. You know, I am actually. I'm not looking for anything serious.

SALLY. That's what I used to tell myself. Convinced I'd die a miserable old dyke.

PETER. And then Diane came along.

SALLY. Yep. I'll still die a miserable old dyke – but at least there'll be two of us!

PETER. And what about the plans for there to be three of you? Any news?

SALLY. We're on the waiting list, so fingers crossed we'll hear soon.

PETER. You know, I've said it before, but if you're really desperate, I would, you know –

SALLY. Yeah, we're not going to risk our kids inheriting your taste in music – or your ears.

PETER. I'm serious.

SALLY. I know you are, and so am I. It's the way your shoulders go all tense when you say 'if you're really desperate' that convinces me it would be a terrible idea, and that you're only saying it to be kind.

PETER. Am I that obvious?

SALLY. Plus the idea of your sperm going into my wife under *any* circumstances – I'm sorry, it's just too weird. Okay?

PETER. Okay.

They smile affectionately.

EDWARD *returns. He looks slightly manic.*

What's happened? You didn't suck him off in the loo, did you?

SALLY. He's a fast worker if he did.

EDWARD. That's not why I'm smiling. I've had an idea.

PETER. Go on…

EDWARD. Now this may sound a little crazy, but hear me out, okay?

PETER. Okay.

EDWARD. Cally –

SALLY. Sally.

EDWARD. Sally – your theatre has sold tickets for an ABBA tribute show in July which can't go ahead, correct?

SALLY. Correct.

EDWARD. Well. I was thinking. (*To* PETER.) Why don't we do it? You and me?

A long beat.

PETER. What?

EDWARD. Well, neither of us is working. You've been sacked –

PETER. Made redundant.

EDWARD. – and I'm a lady of leisure. What about it? You already know all the songs and I'm a fast learner.

SALLY. How would it work? You'd get dressed up in wigs and beards, find a couple of female singers…

EDWARD. No, of course not! Can you imagine me lurking in the shadows?!

PETER. Edward, there are hundreds – probably thousands – of ABBA tribute bands. Diane could just book someone else.

EDWARD. Well she *could*. But we'd be different!

PETER. I don't follow. How would it be different?

EDWARD. We'd be the girls!

SALLY. What?

EDWARD. Why not? Of all the ABBA tribute bands out there, I bet not a single one has men playing Agnetha and Anni-Frid.

PETER. Maybe there's a reason for that. Maybe the world simply isn't crying out for a drag ABBA tribute band.

EDWARD. What have we got to lose?

PETER. Er… Our dignity?

SALLY. You'd be rescuing Diane. It might work, you know.

PETER. Please don't encourage him.

SALLY. I went to a hen party last year. They had an ABBA group. Bloody terrible they were. But if it was done well, by people who really cared and who knew their stuff…

PETER. I refuse to be dragged into Edward's midlife crisis.

SALLY. You could really embrace the gender-bending, you know. If you two are going to be the women, you could get women to be the men.

EDWARD. Male drag! I like it.

SALLY. Who would play who?

PETER. Hang on a minute!

EDWARD. Naturally, I would *have* to be Frida.

SALLY. Which one was she?

EDWARD. The sultry one. The temptress. The flame-haired diva.

SALLY. I thought everyone fancied the blonde?

EDWARD. Straight men have dispiritingly predictable tastes. Of course they were going to plump for the long, blonde hair and the nice bum. Thankfully homosexuals have a rather more sophisticated palate.

SALLY (*pointedly*). Homosexuals do, do they? Actually they were both a bit femme for my taste. Do you have any thoughts on casting, Peter?

PETER. Well, you see, Edward's a tenor, I'm a baritone. Agnetha was a soprano, Frida a mezzo. So strictly speaking, vocally, we should do it the other way round. (*He shakes his head.*) I can't believe I'm even having this conversation.

SALLY. He's going to do it!

PETER. He's not. Are you seriously suggesting we stand on a stage singing ABBA songs – *again*?

EDWARD. Think about it. We can banish the memory of that awful school concert.

PETER. What worries me, Edward, is that the history book on the shelf is *always* repeating itself…

Transition: 'Waterloo' by ABBA.

Scene Four: Dressing Room

June 2015.

SALLY *sits, checking her phone.*

After a few moments, JODIE *bursts in, breathing heavily.*
SALLY *watches her sympathetically.*

SALLY. How did it go?

JODIE. Oh, I got completely the wrong end of the stick. He *is* looking for a Björn and a Benny after all!

SALLY. Yeah, I meant to say.

JODIE. I bet he thinks I'm a complete idiot.

SALLY. I'm sure he doesn't.

JODIE. It'd be playing men. Again. It's weird. Am I giving off some kind of masculine aura, do you think?

SALLY. Take it from me. I've known a lot of butch women in my time. You're not really in the same league.

JODIE. If you say so...

SALLY. How was the octave leap?

JODIE. Didn't even get to do it. He asked me to sing 'Does Your Mother Know' instead. I don't really know that one. The lyrics are a bit creepy, aren't they?

SALLY. I'm sure it went better than you think it did. Do you want a cup of tea, by the way? Kettle's on.

JODIE. Oh, that's kind of you, but I can't hang around.

SALLY. Do you think you would do it if he offered it you?

JODIE. I've had no auditions for months. Well, apart from a commercial casting to play a teabag. And it's two weeks rehearsal fully paid, isn't it?

SALLY. You know it's just a one-off gig, don't you?

JODIE. Oh yes, but I'll take what I can get. I don't really know much about ABBA though. Is that a problem, do you think?

SALLY. Actually that might be for the best. Too many cooks…

JODIE *checks her watch*.

JODIE. I should go. Thanks for being so nice!

JODIE *grabs her bag and as she exits, she bumps into*
EDWARD.

JODIE. Oh, I'm sorry!   EDWARD. Bollocks. Sorry.

EDWARD (*to* SALLY). Hello. One of the auditionees?

SALLY. Yes. Jodie.

EDWARD. How was she?

SALLY. Sweet. Nervous.

EDWARD. Where's Peter?

SALLY. With the last one.

EDWARD. How many have there been?

SALLY. Four. Two cancelled. One no-show.

EDWARD. Right.

SALLY. I thought you were supposed to be sitting in too.

EDWARD. I said I'd do my best. I do have a husband whom
I like to bump into occasionally.

SALLY. This was all your idea.

EDWARD. And now I'm very happy to let Peter run with it.

SALLY. And boy is he doing that. I hope you're properly
committed as well. You're not going to let him down, are
you? This isn't some fad.

EDWARD. No. Of course it isn't.

SALLY. I'm just thinking of Peter. You know how much ABBA
means to him.

EDWARD. You are joking? The first time I ever went round to
his, he insisted on showing me a documentary about them.
He'd watched it umpteen times but he still ended up snivelling

into a tissue when it got to the end and they all split up. They're always making him cry for one reason or another. He was taken to see *ABBA: The Movie* when he was three –

PETER *enters, a large folder under his arm, followed by* MRS CAMPBELL (*Scottish, sixties*).

PETER. Oh, you got here then?

EDWARD. Yes. Sorry. M40 was a nightmare.

PETER. Oh, Edward – this is Mrs Campbell. Mrs Campbell – Edward.

MRS CAMPBELL. Hullo! Lovely to meet you.

She waves at him. A little uncertainly, EDWARD *waves back.*

SALLY. Mrs Campbell's the rehearsal pianist for some of the amateur operatic societies.

PETER. So she very kindly agreed to accompany today's auditionees.

MRS CAMPBELL. I don't really understand what's going on but it does look great fun!

EDWARD. We can but hope! The theatre's very quaint.

PETER. Nice, isn't it? And Diane's said we can use the stage to rehearse.

SALLY. Well – don't keep us in suspense. Have you found your Benny and Björn?

PETER *grimaces.*

PETER. I'm not sure.

MRS CAMPBELL. I have to say: that one you just got rid of – what was she called?

PETER. Faye.

MRS CAMPBELL. Faye, yes, she was *shocking*.

PETER. Well, yes, she kind of was. Although she did have an unusually large upper lip. Which is very Björn, of course.

EDWARD. What did she sing?

PETER. 'Angelo'. I can only assume she got it mixed up with 'Fernando'.

EDWARD. Sacrilege!

SALLY. Why?

PETER. It's The –

PETER/EDWARD. Brotherhood of Man.

MRS CAMPBELL. Now, Lynette – she was my favourite.

PETER. Oh she was the best by far. My only worry is she may be too good.

SALLY. Too good?

PETER. She was a bit cagey. I reckon she might have other irons in the fire.

EDWARD. Well, offer it her and let her decide.

PETER. Hmm. Yeah I think I will.

SALLY. What about Jodie?

EDWARD. She was the one I bumped into?

SALLY. Yeah.

MRS CAMPBELL. Now if I'm perfectly honest, I did find her a wee bit pitchy in her upper register.

SALLY. Really?

MRS CAMPBELL. She could do with engaging her diaphragm more, and her vibrato is rather erratic.

PETER. Yes, it is a bit.

MRS CAMPBELL. And she was shaking like a leaf.

EDWARD. But other than that…?

MRS CAMPBELL. Oh, I liked her.

PETER. Well, I did too, but I didn't really feel she was a Benny.

EDWARD. Too skinny?

SALLY (*dangerously*). I beg your pardon?

EDWARD. Oh come on. I'm not being gratuitously offensive –
for once – but, well, Benny was famously on the… *cuddly*
side, wasn't he?

PETER (*intervening smoothly*). And she can't play the piano
either.

SALLY. Does she need to? Aren't we using backing tracks?

PETER. I suppose so, but it might be nice to have the option.
(*A thought occurs to him*.) Mrs Campbell – are you busy the
next few weeks?

MRS CAMPBELL. No, dear. I thought my sister was coming to
stay but it turns out that was five years ago.

A beat of confusion from all.

EDWARD. I'm sorry?

MRS CAMPBELL. I use the same kitchen calendar every year.
It seems such a waste buying a new one. Well, I looked at the
dates for June and July, and I thought Emily was visiting. I'd
got her room ready and everything. Then the day came for
her to arrive and – nothing! I telephoned her, and she said,
'No, Hermione, that was 2010!'

A beat as they all let this sink in.

PETER. Mrs Campbell, how do you fancy being our Benny?

MRS CAMPBELL. What's that, dear?

PETER. Would you play piano – in the band?

EDWARD (*aside*). Is this wise?

SALLY (*aside*). What's the matter? Is she too skinny as well?

PETER (*to* MRS CAMPBELL). What do you think?

EDWARD (*aside*). Well, no. It's more – when it comes to the
gig, who knows what year she'd turn up?

MRS CAMPBELL. Would I have to sing?

PETER. No, not really. Certainly nothing solo. Benny didn't after all. Well apart from on 'Suzy-Hang-Around', and I don't think we'll be doing that one.

EDWARD. Are you sure about this?

PETER. Of course! Benny just used to smile a lot and bang his head in time to the music. You can manage that, can't you, Mrs C?

MRS CAMPBELL. Well, I'm not sure I really know what I'm letting myself in for, but it sounds like it would be great fun!

PETER. Brilliant! We have our band!

EDWARD. It's like a Cliff Richard film!

SALLY. Oh, I meant to say: Diane was asking if you'd thought up a name. At the moment, the publicity still has all the old details.

EDWARD. How about we do an ABBA and make up a name from our initials? What's your first name again, Mrs C? Naomi, was it?

SALLY (*dryly*). Naomi Campbell?

MRS CAMPBELL. It's Hermione, dear.

EDWARD *thinks for a moment*.

EDWARD. Which gives us… Hermione, Edward, Lynette, Peter.

PETER. But that makes…

SALLY. HELP?

Transition: 'Angelo' by The Brotherhood of Man.

A scratch and it becomes: 'Fernando' by ABBA.

Scene Five: Dressing Room

July 2015.

PETER, EDWARD, *and* MRS CAMPBELL *are sitting in a semicircle.* SALLY *hovers nearby.*

EDWARD. What did she say then?

PETER. Very apologetic, really sorry to let us down, yada-yada-yada. She's been offered Miss Hannigan in *Annie*. Aberystwyth Arts Centre. I *knew* she was hedging her bets.

JODIE enters.

JODIE. Hi everyone! I'm late, aren't I? Am I? Oh I'm not! Not quite! That's a relief. The bus went the wrong way. I think the driver was new. Like me!

She drops her bag on the floor.

SALLY. Don't worry at all. Grab a chair.

PETER. Hi! Welcome!

He shakes her hand.

SALLY. Coffee?

JODIE. Do you have anything herbal?

SALLY. I think there's a packet of rooibos somewhere.

JODIE. Don't worry. I don't want to be difficult! Don't want to be *that* cast member!

She sits next to MRS CAMPBELL.

Hello!

MRS CAMPBELL *waves at her.*

This is great, isn't it? I'm always a bit nervous – first day of a new job. Starting rehearsals! But it's exciting too. I'd given up on this, if I'm honest. When you didn't call, I thought: oh well, they've obviously asked someone else. Only chance I've got now is if their first choice turns it down. And then you rang after all. So, is that what happened? Was I the back-up?

An awkward pause.

PETER. No! No, not at all.

JODIE. I don't mind. I probably wouldn't have hired me either! I forgot my Rescue Remedy. Did I mention that?

SALLY. Shall we go round and introduce ourselves? I'm Sally: I'm your stage manager for the show.

PETER. I'm Peter. I'm playing Agnetha.

EDWARD. Edward. I shall be embodying, for the entertainment of one and all, Her Serene Highness Princess Anni-Frid Synni Lyngstad-Fredriksson-Andersson-Reuss, Dowager Countess of Plauen.

A beat.

SALLY. Come again?

PETER (*sighing*). That is actually Frida's official title. She married a prince. It's a long story.

SALLY. Okay...

JODIE. I'm Jodie Milligan, AKA Björn Ulvaeus. Did I get that right?

PETER. Spot on.

They look expectantly at MRS CAMPBELL *who smiles at them all.*

MRS CAMPBELL. Oh. It's my turn, is it? I'm Mrs Campbell. And I think this is going to be a lot of fun!

PETER. Mrs Campbell is our Benny.

MRS CAMPBELL. Yes. Yes, that's right.

PETER. Right: the good-slash-scary news first. The concert is the 11th July. A week on Saturday.

SALLY. We're pretty much sold out already but Diane has some tickets held back if you want some for friends and family. Just let me know.

JODIE. Ooh – exciting!

PETER. We've got about an hour and a half to fill – so I reckon we need to have about fifteen songs ready by then. I know that sounds a lot but I think it's doable. Now, I've made little folders for you all…

He hands folders around to them all.

I thought we could open with 'Waterloo', followed by the disco tracks, then some ballads, finishing with 'Thank You for the Music' and then 'Dancing Queen' as an encore.

EDWARD. Hang on, you haven't got 'The Winner Takes It All' on this list.

PETER. We can't do them all.

EDWARD. But it's my favourite.

PETER. It's to balance it out. Otherwise I've got more solos than you.

EDWARD. Then I'll sing it.

PETER. I – and any self-respecting ABBA fan – would find it profoundly triggering for an Agnetha lead to be sung by Frida. Or vice versa.

SALLY. Do you not think they're going to be triggered by Agnetha and Frida being men?

EDWARD. Swap one of the other numbers out then.

PETER. Listen, Edward. Nobody can sing 'The Winner Takes It All' like Agnetha Fältskog, therefore nobody else should even try. Certainly not me.

EDWARD. What about Meryl?

JODIE. Who's Meryl?

EDWARD. Who's Meryl!

PETER. She attempts it in 'The Film That We Will Never Name'. Like I said, nobody else should even try.

EDWARD. At least 'The Day Before You Came' isn't on the list.

PETER. It's an amazing song!

EDWARD. It's six minutes long and it has no chorus. I refuse to discuss it any further.

JODIE. Can I ask a question? Have you booked a dialect coach?

PETER. I'm sorry?

JODIE. I don't want to sound full of myself, but my Swedish accent is pretty good. I can probably help out if you don't want to hire someone specially.

PETER. I don't really want to do the comedy accents. I don't want us to take the piss.

EDWARD (*ironically*). Quite. It's important the audience takes this as seriously as Peter does.

PETER. Look, I'm not saying we can't have fun, but I'd like it to be affectionate.

JODIE. Well, the offer's there if you want it.

MRS CAMPBELL *leafs through the folder.*

MRS CAMPBELL. Oh, there's even a *glossary* at the back! I do love a glossary.

PETER. Well, you know, I thought – if there are any useful facts or names you're unfamiliar with –

MRS CAMPBELL (*peering at the folder*). Moaner. No clit.

SALLY. I'm sorry?   JODIE. Pardon?!   EDWARD. Ha!

PETER. It's Benny's second wife. It's pronounced 'Mona Noerklit'.

MRS CAMPBELL. The poor woman. You'd change it, wouldn't you? Will they not let you do that in Sweden?

SALLY. Talking of names, Diane's still asking what she's supposed to call you.

PETER. Ah yes. I thought we could come up with something together!

EDWARD. It's not a complete dictatorship then.

JODIE. Dancing Queens?

PETER. There have been ABBA tribute bands for over twenty years now, Jodie. Sadly Dancing Queen was nabbed long ago. Now, on page eight of your packs, you'll see some others that have already been taken.

They all dutifully turn over their sheets.

MRS CAMPBELL. Oh my! Aren't there a lot of them? Swede Dreams. That's actually quite clever!

EDWARD. Björn Again, of course, ABBA Rebjörn, The Björn Identity…

JODIE. ABBAtastic, ABBAwhelming, ABBAsolutely…

SALLY. BABA, FABBA, FLABBA… FLABBA?

PETER. Their USP is that they are… plus-size.

EDWARD (*amused*). Oh, that's –

SALLY. Offensive.

EDWARD. You read my mind.

JODIE. So if *our* USP is ABBA in drag…

MRS CAMPBELL. DRABBA?

PETER. That's an… idea, Mrs C.

SALLY. And presumably these are the ones actually named after ABBA songs…

PETER. Yep. There's a Voulez-Vous, Super Troupers, Take a Chance On Us… many, many more.

EDWARD. What does that leave us with?

PETER. Well I thought, given the whole concept: what about 'I Am Just a Girl'?

SALLY. What's that got to do with ABBA?

PETER. It was on *Ring Ring* – their 1973 debut album. I mean strictly speaking, they weren't even ABBA then – they were still called Benny & Björn, Agnetha & Frida, but I think we can get away with it.

EDWARD. Peter, that is one of the worst ideas I've ever heard. We can't name ourselves after an obscure album track.

JODIE. Any other options?

PETER. Well, on page fourteen, you'll find a list of every song they ever recorded.

They flip through the pages and scan the list.

SALLY. You're right. All the good ones have gone.

EDWARD. Oh, I don't know. There are a few that seem appropriate at the present moment: 'Why Did It Have to Be Me'? 'Disillusion'? 'Should I Laugh or Cry'?

JODIE. I like 'Disillusion'. It could be, like, 'This Illusion'. (*Sounding 'street'*.) 'Dis Illusion'. Yeah?

PETER. It's another *Ring Ring* album track. Does that matter?

EDWARD. I can't help feeling we want something with a teensy bit more brand recognition.

SALLY. What about Head Over Heels…?

EDWARD. It's hardly their biggest hit.

PETER. It got to number twenty-five.

EDWARD. Ah yes. The coveted 'number twenty-five' spot.

PETER. ABBA does tango. Which, incidentally, was the working title for the song.

EDWARD. I apologise. This is what the next two weeks are going to be like.

PETER. Interestingly, the working title of 'Fernando' was also 'Tango' –

EDWARD. Redefining 'interesting' for you there, ladies.

PETER. Although it suits 'Head Over Heels' far better.

EDWARD. Jesus Christ, Peter! Make it stop!

PETER. Sorry. Got carried away.

JODIE. It kind of fits, doesn't it? We're turning the concept of an ABBA tribute band on its head.

EDWARD. I don't object to it.

SALLY. I'll let Diane know straight away!

MRS CAMPBELL. And we'll be wearing heels!

Beat.

Won't we?

Transition: 'Head Over Heels' by ABBA.

Scene Six: The Stage

July 2015

PETER *has his folder open and is showing* SALLY *costume designs.* MRS CAMPBELL *is peering over as well.*

PETER. So, I've been trying to narrow it down to the most iconic looks through the years. I've got it down to four – the Eurovision costumes: Frida in her long, orange skirt and Agnetha with the little blue crocheted cap; the yellow and blue 'cat' dresses; the '79 live tour striped bodysuits; and the white evening dresses from 'Super Trouper'.

SALLY. Peter. We have less than a fortnight. Choose one.

JODIE *enters and joins them.*

MRS CAMPBELL. These are our uniforms. Aren't they fancy?

JODIE. Crikey. That's a *lot* of lycra.

MRS CAMPBELL. Yes… and it is quite an *unforgiving* fabric, isn't it? Will we not all have our lumps and bumps showing in all the wrong places? I mean, I don't want to be personal but…

MRS CAMPBELL *gestures to* PETER*'s crotch.*

SALLY. We just have to get the upholstery right, that's all.

MRS CAMPBELL. If you say so, Sally! I'm sure it's all in your very capable hands.

MRS CAMPBELL *goes to sit at the keyboard, adjusts her glasses and studies her sheet music.*

JODIE (*sotto voce*). I don't want to be funny – but is she going to do it like that?

SALLY. Not sure.

PETER. Mrs Campbell, on the day, do you think you'll be able to do it without the glasses?

MRS CAMPBELL. But without my spectacles, I can't read the music.

SALLY. We do have backing tracks. We don't really need you to play live, you know.

MRS CAMPBELL. Then what am I meant to be doing?

PETER. Remember what we said? About the smiling? And the head-banging?

MRS CAMPBELL *smiles uncertainly.*

JODIE. Where's Edward?

SALLY. He's being all mysterious. Said he had something to show us.

PETER. God help us.

JODIE. I'm still a bit nervous about Mrs C.

SALLY. I think she'll be fine. All we really need behind that keyboard is a vaguely human shape. As long as they're wearing a beard…

PETER. The girls did used to get all the attention, I'm afraid. It might be a bit of a thankless task: being Björn. You're not regretting it, are you, Jodie?

JODIE. Oh, no, not at all. What would I be doing instead? Just my temping job. Or the odd day as an extra on *Doctors*. I'd be standing there watching Dr Zara, thinking, maybe one day: if I work hard and I get my break, that could be me. But in the meantime, every day I get to be on stage, I know it's one more day where I've carried on, and not given up on my dream. I'm still performing. Still doing it.

SALLY. Did you ever hear back about the teabag?

JODIE. Yes. They went in another direction.

EDWARD (*offstage*). Okay. Are you all ready for this?

SALLY. Ready as we'll ever be.

JODIE *and* PETER *move to sit downstage.*

EDWARD (*offstage*). Can I have a blackout on stage, please?

SALLY (*sighing*). Coming right up.

SALLY *exits. A moment later the stage is plunged into darkness.*

EDWARD. Spotlight!

SALLY. You'll get what you're given.

A light hits EDWARD, *now centre-stage. He has a sweater wrapped around his waist as a make-shift skirt. He has his back to the audience.*

EDWARD. And – cue the track!

The instrumental track begins. EDWARD *turns slowly to face the audience, and then begins to do a jazz ballet solo. It's practically identical to the solo Frida performed in the*

1979 tour: fist punches, high kicks, twirls, leaps, spinning on the spot.

EDWARD *camps it up outrageously. At the end, he drops to the floor, as if spent.*

SALLY. Are you done?

EDWARD (*from his dying swan position*). It is finished.

The lights come up slowly. PETER *looks perturbed.* SALLY *looks skeptical.* JODIE *is still giggling.* MRS CAMPBELL *beams and applauds furiously.*

MRS CAMPBELL. Bravo! Brava?

SALLY. What was that?

JODIE. I think I might have done a little wee…

She checks.

No. No, I think I'm okay.

EDWARD (*raising his head*). That, Sally, was an authentic recreation of Frida's dance solo during the instrumental break of 'Gimme! Gimme! Gimme! – brackets – A Man After Midnight – close brackets' from ABBA's 1979 world tour. Found it on YouTube.

He stands.

SALLY. I see.

JODIE. No offence, but when *she* did it, was it really… that bad?

EDWARD. They had the voices of angels, Josie –

JODIE. Jodie.

EDWARD. Jodie. But neither of our ladies had what you would call 'natural rhythm'.

PETER. The difference was, you could sort of tell Agnetha knew she couldn't dance. Frida's tragedy was she thought she could.

EDWARD. Well, does it go in the show?

PETER. You know I don't want to take the piss…

EDWARD. Peter. I know how you feel about them, believe me, and I respect that and I love you for it, I really do. But at the end of the day, we're two middle-aged poofs prancing about in platform heels and shimmery tights. Jodie here may not have wet herself – but I think you should be prepared that our audience just might…

Transition: 'Gimme! Gimme! Gimme! (A Man After Midnight)' by ABBA.

Scene Seven: Male Dressing Room

11 July 2015.

PETER *sits at a dressing table. He is wearing a dressing gown and has a stocking cap on his head.*

He picks up a foundation stick and starts to apply it to his face. He peers into the mirror.

EDWARD *enters. He is dressed identically. He sits next to* PETER *at the dressing table.*

They look at one another.

EDWARD. How are you feeling?

PETER. Bit nervous. You?

EDWARD. What's the worst that can happen?

PETER. Well –

EDWARD. Don't answer that. Let's talk about something else.

PETER. I'm up for that.

They both start to apply their make-up.

EDWARD. You ever done drag before?

PETER. Never. You?

EDWARD. A few times. Freshers' week at uni. Occasional fancy-dress parties. Melvyn and I went to one once as Batman and Catwoman.

PETER. Really? Which version? Julie Newmar? Eartha Kitt?

EDWARD. Michelle Pfeiffer.

PETER. Bloody hell. The full rubber-catsuit look?

EDWARD. It was very sweaty, but I looked amazing. And afterwards, Melvyn and I had the best sex we've ever had.

PETER. Aw that's nice. You'll have to show me the photos one day. (*Quickly.*) I meant of the costumes, not of the –

EDWARD. I know what you meant.

They continue in silence for a moment.

PETER. I'm a bit worried I'm going to be less Agnetha, more Ann Widdecombe.

EDWARD. I just know I'm going to look like my mother. How depressing is that?

PETER. Shall we just slap it all on?

EDWARD. The seventies were not subtle. What colours are you using?

PETER. Frosted pink lips, and lots and *lots* of blue eyeshadow.

EDWARD. Of course. Classic Agnetha. I'm going for grey-green round the eyes and for the lips – (*He checks the lipstick label.*) scandalous scarlet.

PETER. Are you going to try contouring?

EDWARD. I wouldn't know where to begin.

EDWARD *reaches into his bag and pulls out a can of gin and tonic. He opens it.*

Want one?

PETER. Before the show? Bit dangerous, isn't it?

EDWARD. I'm only having one.

Beat.

Talking of amazing sex, have you... had any... recently?

PETER. Are you kidding? I've been too busy. Grindr is feeling very neglected.

EDWARD. I bet Nick Clegg's kicking himself. He has all that free time now as well...

PETER. Have you gone on it again?

EDWARD. Are *you* kidding? I've learned my lesson. You were definitely a sign. The Almighty kiboshed Grindr once. I don't need to be told twice.

PETER. How's Melvyn? Is absence making the heart grow fonder?

EDWARD. You know, it is. God knows what got into me. To think I could have risked everything just for – well, for a brief dalliance with a man with hairy toenails.

PETER. Self-sabotage. You wouldn't be the first.

EDWARD. I'm not cut out for infidelity. Or maybe it's just living under the same roof as my mother again that makes me yearn for Melvyn and home. Mother's not been right since they cancelled *Bergerac*.

PETER. You know John Nettles played King Rat here in 1993?

EDWARD. I didn't but I bet you she does.

PETER. Is she watching tonight?

EDWARD. She is. You know, after all these years, I think she's actually embraced the worst. Her sexually deviant child has landed her with a son-in-law who's five years older than she is. Watching me prance around on stage, singing disco anthems in drag – it's pretty small beer really.

PETER. The ostrich is finally taking its head out of the sand!

EDWARD. I'm not sure I'd go quite that far.

They continue to apply make-up.

What about you? Is your nan coming?

PETER. No.

EDWARD. Does she even know we're doing it?

PETER. She knows I'm singing with the obnoxious kid I used to bring home with me for tea. No more than that.

EDWARD. Seems a pity. All those years of you subjecting her to ABBA: can't she bear to listen to them any more?

PETER. It's not that.

EDWARD. So what is it then?

PETER. It's all just a bit – a bit –

EDWARD. What? Gay?

PETER. I told you before. Unless I'm introducing her to a boyfriend, what's the point of upsetting her? At her age…

EDWARD. Who says she'll be upset? Look, Peter, don't you think this is a bit pathetic? You won't let her see the show because you're still lurking in the closet!

PETER. You don't understand.

EDWARD. Is Sally out to her family?

PETER. Yeah. Of course.

EDWARD. And does she think you should tell your nan?

PETER. She minds her own business.

EDWARD. Ha! I'll believe that when I see it.

PETER *crosses to a shelf and fetches a wig block with his blonde wig.*

PETER. I thought you two were getting on alright.

EDWARD. We tolerate each other.

PETER. You know, there's something I've never told you.

EDWARD. Oh God. You're not going to declare your undying love for me? If you are, your timing's really lousy.

PETER. Don't flatter yourself. No, I've never told you how brave I think you were. I'll always remember you telling me how it felt when you got expelled: being paraded in front of everyone. All of them pointing and sniggering because you'd dared to tell another boy that you liked him.

EDWARD. Funny, isn't it? How shame lingers...

PETER. Do you remember Mr Ditchfield? At school?

EDWARD. Of course. Taught maths. Looked like a penguin.

PETER. That's right. He warned me to stay away from you. Told me you weren't a good influence.

EDWARD. Really?

PETER. He told me about why you had to leave St Augustine's long before you did. The whole Barney Bailey scandal. Advised me to steer clear in case you tried something on with me too.

EDWARD. What a bastard!

PETER. I know.

EDWARD. But you didn't. Steer clear.

PETER. No. I didn't.

EDWARD. At least not on that occasion...

PETER. What do you mean?

EDWARD. Things changed after Elizabeth Frost got her slobbery chops around you.

PETER. She was my first girlfriend. I got carried away.

EDWARD. Well, I got you back in the end!

EDWARD *touches* PETER's *hand*. PETER *smiles*.

After a moment, EDWARD *catches sight of himself in the mirror.*

Oh bollocks. Will you look at my eyelashes? How on earth are you supposed to get them symmetrical? I look as if I've had a stroke... TWO STROKES! (*Looking around the room.*) Why are there no sinks in here? Who designs a bloody dressing room and doesn't put a bloody sink in it? I'm going to the bathroom.

EDWARD *stands and moves to the exit.*

I don't believe for a minute that John Nettles stood for this.

He goes to leave. Suddenly remembers his can of gin and tonic, returns for it, and exits.

A beat.

PETER *smiles again and puts the finishing touches to his make-up. He thinks. He gets his mobile out. He dials and switches the phone to speaker. It rings.* NAN *answers.*

NAN (*voice-over*). Hello?

PETER. Hi, Nan. It's me.

NAN (*voice-over*). Oh hello, love. Everything alright?

PETER. Yes. Yes. Everything's fine. I'm just at the Library Theatre. About to do this concert thing with Edward...

NAN (*voice-over*). Yes, dear. The thing you don't think is my cup of tea.

PETER. Well, I was thinking again. And I thought maybe you might enjoy it after all. We're doing a sort of ABBA thing.

NAN (*voice-over*). That's lovely. You and your ABBA...

PETER. I've got a spare ticket. It starts at eight.

NAN (*voice-over*). You know I'd love to, Peter. But I don't think I can get down there in time.

PETER. You've got forty-five minutes. Call a taxi. I'll pay.

NAN (*voice-over*). Oh that's very extravagant! Are you sure? I'll feel like the Queen.

PETER. No less than you deserve, Nan.

A beat.

NAN (*voice-over*). Anything else, love?

PETER. Erm. Well, yes, Nan, actually I think there is.

NAN (*voice-over*). Oh?

PETER. Are you sitting down?

NAN (*voice-over*). Do I need to be?

PETER. Probably not a bad idea.

NAN (*voice-over*). Okay. Let me just move Molly off the armchair. Molly – down… Come on, Molly. Get down… Down… Down, Molly.

PETER *sighs and raises his eyes to the sky.*

There's a good girl. Now, what's this all about?

PETER. It's something I should have told you a long time ago. I've wanted to but I guess I've been too scared. Scared that you'd be worried or upset, or that things between us wouldn't be the same. But it's important that you know.

NAN (*voice-over*). Alright…

PETER. I like… that is, as well as girls, I'm *attracted* to, well, boys. As well. As girls. So, that's kind of it. I like boys and girls. I mean, romantically. And, I guess, sexually too…

NAN (*voice-over*). Right. Anything else?

PETER. Anything else…?

NAN (*voice-over*). Honestly, you are daft sometimes. Why would you think a little thing like that would change things between us, Peter? I'm just glad you've decided to tell me now. Before it's too late.

PETER. Oh, Nan. I love you.

NAN (*voice-over*). I love you too, my darling.

A knock on the door.

PETER. I'd better go. We'll speak properly later. Call that cab!

NAN (*voice-over*). I will, dear. Good luck!

She hangs up.

PETER. Come in!

SALLY *enters.*

SALLY. How's it going?

PETER. Nearly ready. Jodie and Mrs C alright?

SALLY. I've just stuck Mrs Campbell's beard on. There's a sentence I never thought I'd say.

PETER *laughs.*

Are you looking forward to it?

PETER. I think so. Who'd have thought? Librarian to drag queen in less than a month!

SALLY. It sounds like a BBC3 reality show…

PETER. Don't let on to Edward, but I think this has actually done me good, you know.

SALLY. Are you sure you're okay?

PETER. Yeah, I've just – Er yeah, I'm fine. Honestly.

SALLY *hugs him.* EDWARD *enters.*

EDWARD. Oh – am I interrupting something?

SALLY *and* PETER *part.*

SALLY. Not at all. I just came in to say break a leg. You ladies go out there and give 'em hell.

She exits. EDWARD *and* PETER *squeeze each other's hands and then return to their 'spots' to complete their make-up.*

Lights narrow to focus on the two wig blocks: one red wig, one blonde wig.

Then a blackout.

Transition: 'Super Trouper' by ABBA.

End of Act One.

ACT TWO

Scene One: Female Dressing Room

Transition: 'Take a Chance On Me' (Live) by ABBA.

11 July 2015.

JODIE *bursts into the room, in a state of exuberant excitement. She is in costume as Björn, her wig in her hand.* SALLY *and* MRS CAMPBELL *(in her Benny costume, peeling off her beard) follow.*

JODIE. Oh my God, I went completely blank. That whole second verse. I think I just went 'Mer-ner-mer. Ner-mer-ner.'

SALLY. Don't worry. They'll think you were doing it in Swedish. Here. Let me take that.

SALLY *takes the wig.*

Did you enjoy it, Mrs C?

MRS CAMPBELL. Oh yes, it was great fun!

JODIE. They *really* loved your 'Soo-pah-pah troo-pah-pahs'!

MRS CAMPBELL. I know. Who'd have thought!

JODIE. And the head-banging!

MRS CAMPBELL. I got a bit carried away... I might just grab a couple of aspirin.

She goes to her 'spot' and gets some tablets from her handbag.

SALLY. Sorry about the delay with the cueing. 'Fernando' was waiting a hell of a time before he heard those bloody drums.

A knock on the door and EDWARD *enters: a dressing gown over his costume, a Waitrose bag in his hand.*

EDWARD. Well, gentlemen – and lesbian – I think we got away with it.

He gives JODIE *a hug.*

JODIE. You were amazing!

SALLY (*unseen by* EDWARD) *makes a gesture of an expanding head exploding.*

EDWARD. Oh please. I was hardly that…

A mobile buzzes. JODIE *crosses to her dressing table and fishes it out of her bag.*

EDWARD *takes* MRS CAMPBELL*'s hand and kisses it.*

Congratulations, hubby.

MRS CAMPBELL. Oh, Edward. You charmer!

JODIE (*checking her phone*). Oh poo! I could have sworn I'd booked the right number of tickets.

EDWARD *produces a bottle of champagne and five plastic flutes from his bag. He sets about opening the bottle.*

SALLY. Did some of your lot not get in?

JODIE. They squeezed them in at the back. Oh, I'll never hear the end of this.

Another knock at the door.

PETER (*offstage*). Are you decent?

EDWARD. Never, but come in anyway.

PETER *enters, gowned.*

PETER. Sorry, everyone. I was putting Nan in a taxi.

EDWARD (*a little smug*). And what did she think? Was it her cup of tea after all?

PETER. She had tears in her eyes. But I think that's a good sign.

Champagne pops. JODIE *hugs* PETER.

JODIE. What a buzz, eh?

PETER. That's one word for it. One way or another, it's been a hell of an evening.

EDWARD *pours out the champagne and starts handing round the glasses.*

EDWARD. No jeering schoolkids this time. *Has* the history book been rewritten then?

PETER. I'm not sure. I think I'm still in a state of shock.

MRS CAMPBELL. Not for me, thank you.

EDWARD. You'll have a *spot*, surely, Mrs C?

MRS CAMPBELL (*holding up the aspirin packet*). I don't think I should mix drugs and alcohol.

EDWARD (*moving on*). If you're sure.

MRS CAMPBELL (*quickly*). Well, maybe just a wee smidge!

EDWARD *pours and then raises his own glass.*

EDWARD. Here's to us!

PETER. One more toast, and then we'll pay the bill!

SALLY (*in mock desperation*). *Please*, no more quotes!

EDWARD. Here's to Head Over Heels.

ALL. Head Over Heels!

CHRISTIAN (*twenties, Australian*) *enters. They turn in surprise.*

CHRISTIAN. Oh, hi. I'm sorry. I was looking for the stage door. And they sent me through here. I didn't realise –

SALLY (*brusquely*). Yeah, there isn't really a stage door. People tend to wait in the foyer.

CHRISTIAN. I'm really sorry. I'll just –

He goes to leave.

EDWARD (*swiftly*). Oh, that's okay. I mean – now you're here.

SALLY *rolls her eyes*.

CHRISTIAN. I don't want to intrude.

EDWARD. Nonsense. Bubbly?

EDWARD looks around for another glass. Can't see one. He sees MRS CAMPBELL has yet to drink from hers, so he swipes it from her and hands it to CHRISTIAN. MRS CAMPBELL looks a little forlorn.

CHRISTIAN. Oh, right. Well, yes. Thanks. That's really kind of you.

JODIE. Did you watch the show?

CHRISTIAN. Yes, I did.

PETER (*grimacing*). Our apologies.

CHRISTIAN. It was only your first gig, right?

EDWARD. First and last.

CHRISTIAN. Oh? That's a pity.

JODIE. What makes you say that?

CHRISTIAN. Well, to do all that work. Just for one night. I've seen a *lot* of ABBA tribute bands and believe me I've seen a lot worse.

SALLY. Maybe we could put that on a poster: 'I've seen a lot worse'…

CHRISTIAN. No, seriously. I think you could have something here. It's a really fun concept.

PETER. Really?

SALLY. I'm sorry, but who are you?

CHRISTIAN. Oh, right, yeah. My name's Christian. Christian Sanderson. Did you guys know that Christian is actually Björn's middle name? And Sanderson is an anagram of Andersson, because Benny's surname has a double 's'…

A beat.

SALLY (*to* JODIE, *under her breath*). I think we've got another one in the building…

CHRISTIAN. I'm a big ABBA fan.

SALLY. You don't say…

JODIE. Peter's *our* resident ABBA geek.

CHRISTIAN. I thought at least one of you must be. Some of the little details: Agnetha biting her lower lip; Frida's wig flying off.

EDWARD. That wasn't entirely deliberate…

CHRISTIAN. I run a Facebook group: ABBA Chat. Maybe I could add you guys…

PETER. Oh, I'm not on Facebook.

JODIE. What do you chat about?

CHRISTIAN. Oh, all sorts: ABBA, *Chess*, the Hootenanny Singers.

SALLY. The Hootey-who?

PETER. Björn's sixties skiffle band.

MRS CAMPBELL. It's in the glossary.

CHRISTIAN. Admittedly, sometimes it can get a bit heated! 'Frida was the better singer!'; 'No, Agnetha was!' (*He chuckles indulgently.*) But I generally manage to keep the peace. We have occasional real-life meet-ups too. And I go and see as many tribute bands as I can and then I post reviews for everyone in the group.

EDWARD. So if I ply you with more champers, will you say nice things about us?

CHRISTIAN. Ha! I'm always honest with my reviews. But I'd write nice things about you guys anyway.

PETER. Do you think that some fans might not like the idea – you know, think we were being disrespectful?

CHRISTIAN. You've gotta have a sense of humour, haven't you? I mean, nobody loves ABBA more than me – but personally speaking, I try not to take myself or them too seriously. A couple of the guys in the group are a bit intense. I mean – they're not quite on the Gert van der Graaf scale, but you know, they're not far off.

CHRISTIAN, PETER *and* MRS CAMPBELL *chuckle. The others look nonplussed.*

MRS CAMPBELL. Did none of you read your glossary? He was the blonde lassie's stalker in the late nineties. He bought a hut on her private island in the Swedish archipelago. He ended up scooping up her poo from –

EDWARD (*quickly*). Have you come far? I assume you haven't actually flown in from Australia just to see us.

CHRISTIAN. Ha! No, not quite that bad. Just from Sheffield.

MRS CAMPBELL *gets up and exits* (*presumably to the toilet!*).

EDWARD. And do you have to get back there tonight?

CHRISTIAN. No, I'm booked into a B&B.

EDWARD. Great. Do you fancy coming out for a drink? We are going to celebrate, aren't we?

SALLY. I can't, I'm afraid. Diane's knackered. She's had to deal with a few audience complaints. People who booked ages ago who weren't expecting the gender-swapped version.

EDWARD. Homophobes.

SALLY. She's having to refund their 'Money, Money, Money'. Oh bloody hell, now you've got me doing it!

EDWARD. What about you, Jodie?

JODIE. I don't think I can. I've got a bunch of people in. And I'm on a bit of a budget. I can't really afford –

EDWARD. My treat.

CHRISTIAN. I don't want to monopolise you. Your adoring public will be dying to get their hands on you.

EDWARD. Don't worry about that. I can see my mother off very swiftly. In fact, that happens to be a persistent fantasy of mine.

CHRISTIAN. I've taken up too much of your time already. But in my humble opinion, for what it's worth, I think you should carry on. And if you do, and I hope this isn't being too pushy, I'm a photographer. I'd love to take some publicity shots for you. Mates' rates obvs. Here's my card.

He hands it to PETER.

PETER. That's very kind of you.

CHRISTIAN. I can always promote you on ABBA Chat as well. Look, I'm gonna go. But really, guys – well done.

He shakes all their hands one by one and exits.

Silence.

SALLY. Okay, ladies. You can roll your tongues in now.

PETER. What? Oh no, he's a child.

EDWARD. He may be a child but he's a bloody gorgeous one.

SALLY. Don't you have a husband?

EDWARD. I can window-shop!

JODIE. Oh, don't start bickering! You heard him – our public awaits! (*She glances around.*) Mrs Campbell, are you coming?

MRS CAMPBELL *appears: a new bottle of champagne and a mug in one hand.*

MRS CAMPBELL. This is very moreish, you know. Did someone say we were going out partying?

Transition: 'On and On and On' by ABBA.

Scene Two: The Stage

September 2015.

Professional camera lighting and equipment is scattered around the stage, as is an electric guitar and keyboards.

CHRISTIAN *is fiddling with his camera.* JODIE *is in full Björn costume – including wig.*

JODIE (*calling into the corridor*). Okay, I'll tell him!

(*To* CHRISTIAN.) Sally's just fixing Mrs Campbell's beard. It's such a relief that I don't have to worry about facial hair. Well, Björn's anyway!

CHRISTIAN. Although Björn did of course grow a beard in the eighties. He's had one ever since, in fact.

JODIE. Now, I did not know that. That's bad, isn't it? A gap in my research.

CHRISTIAN. Would it make a difference to what you do on stage?

JODIE. I was more thorough with my character work when I was at drama school. I've got sloppy.

CHRISTIAN. Well, I admire your commitment.

SALLY *enters.*

SALLY. Thanks for coming down to do this, Christian.

CHRISTIAN. Believe me, the pleasure is all mine. I was so stoked to get Peter's call.

JODIE. To be honest, I think it was you being so nice that convinced him to carry on. It made a difference hearing it from another proper fan.

CHRISTIAN. Then we're all happy! I never thought I'd get to do an actual photoshoot with ABBA! Or as close as I'll ever get.

JODIE. Isn't it weird being a fan of a group who split up before you were even born?

CHRISTIAN. I've never really thought of it like that. At least you know you're never gonna be disappointed by their new material, huh?

JODIE. I suppose so. Do you think they ever would get back together?

CHRISTIAN. They want people to remember them as they were: young and energetic. And I respect that. Besides, they've got guys like you to keep the memories alive!

SALLY. Or obliterate them completely…

MRS CAMPBELL *enters, fully costumed, wigged and bearded.*

CHRISTIAN (*à la Jack Nicholson*). Heeeere's Benny!

MRS CAMPBELL. I'm sorry to be so long. The beard's not sticking at all well. I think the glue's gone off. At least I hope it's that. If it's not, there's a very peculiar smell coming from somewhere. (*She sniffs her armpits.*) I don't *think* it's me.

CHRISTIAN. I'll keep an eye on the beard. Right. Shall we get started? We could be waiting all day for the ladies to join us!

MRS CAMPBELL. You know, I'm happy being in the background.

JODIE. Come on, Mrs C. Let's enjoy our moment in the spotlight!

CHRISTIAN. Why don't you grab your instruments?

SALLY *helps* MRS CAMPBELL *with the keyboards and* JODIE *fetches her guitar.*

MRS CAMPBELL *glances down at her bosom and then eyes* JODIE*'s breasts appreciatively…*

JODIE (*suddenly self-conscious*). What? What's the matter?

MRS CAMPBELL. You can tell you're a proper professional actress, you know. You really go the extra mile.

JODIE. I'm sorry?

MRS CAMPBELL (*sotto voce*). What do you use?

JODIE. Use for what?

MRS CAMPBELL. You know… to strap down your…

> MRS CAMPBELL *mimes two hefty melons.* JODIE *looks down sadly at her chest.*

JODIE. Nothing.

> *The two of them pose for the camera:* JODIE *still a bit self-conscious,* MRS CAMPBELL *starts to enjoy herself.*

CHRISTIAN. Do you think we could lose the glasses, Mrs Campbell? Can you manage without them?

MRS CAMPBELL. Would you mind, Sally?

> *She hands the glasses to* SALLY.

CHRISTIAN. There you go!

> *He clicks away, chatting as he does so.*

> You know, I think you guys have put such a clever spin on the original dynamic. After all, ABBA have always had this magical appeal to the LGBT+ community.

JODIE. I wonder why that is.

CHRISTIAN. Oh, I could give you my full thesis on the social and cultural significance of ABBA and their synergy with the queer experience.

MRS CAMPBELL. Oh yes?

CHRISTIAN. I mean, I won't. Don't look so worried.

MRS CAMPBELL. Right.

CHRISTIAN. It is ironic, though, don't you think? ABBA were two straight couples, and here are you guys: two *gay* couples – with Mrs Campbell tagging along as the token hetero, of course! Let's just hope you don't all end up splitting up, eh?

> *A beat while this sinks in.*

SALLY. Erm. We're not two couples, you know.

CHRISTIAN *stops clicking*.

CHRISTIAN. You're not? Really? I thought the four of you were –

SALLY. You thought wrong. I mean, well, I suppose three of us are on the 'rainbow spectrum', but Jodie here –

JODIE. Oh no, I'm not gay – I just can't get a boyfriend.

MRS CAMPBELL. Why would you not include me?

CHRISTIAN. Excuse me?

MRS CAMPBELL. As part of your 'queer synergy'.

CHRISTIAN. Oh, I'm sorry. I just assumed. 'Mrs' Campbell… Are you… gay?

MRS CAMPBELL. Well, no. But it would be nice to think the option were available to me.

CHRISTIAN. So, Edward and Peter – they're not together either?

SALLY. Nope. Just very old friends. Peter's a confirmed bachelor. Edward has a husband.

JODIE. He came up to see the last gig we did. In the pub. He's older than Edward but he was really sweet.

MRS CAMPBELL. Like a *kindly* Michael Palin.

JODIE. Is Michael Palin *not* kind then, do you think?

MRS CAMPBELL. I don't know, dear. I've always found him a bit unsettling. All that travelling. What's he running from?

JODIE. Oh, but he always seems so nice.

MRS CAMPBELL. Yes.

JODIE. So?

MRS CAMPBELL. Too nice.

CHRISTIAN. Well, I apologise for my faux pas!

EDWARD *and* PETER *enter, resplendent in their Frida and Agnetha drag.*

EDWARD. 'Faux pas'? Is someone bad-mouthing my dance steps again?

SALLY. The Ugly Sisters have arrived.

EDWARD. Shut it, you, or you'll be sweeping cinders and we won't let you go to the ball.

SALLY. Trust me, Edward, your balls hold no interest for me whatsoever.

CHRISTIAN. I'm loving the new outfits!

PETER. Thank you. Now we're extending the show, Sally's said I can have more than one set of costumes.

CHRISTIAN. What songs are you adding?

PETER. Some of the later stuff: you know, from '81 and '82.

EDWARD. Although I drew the line at letting him sing 'The Day Before You Came'.

PETER. Let's not start that again.

EDWARD. Forgive us, Christian. We've been having this same argument for nearly thirty years.

CHRISTIAN (*quietly*). It's one of my favourites.

PETER *shoots him a quick smile*. CHRISTIAN *winks at him*.

PETER. I also want to look at some extra wigs.

EDWARD. I can tell you now: that purple, spiky atrocity is going nowhere near my head.

PETER (*explaining to the others*). Frida got her hair cut short when she got divorced. It was kind of her 'Fuck you, Benny' look.

EDWARD. She must have been extremely traumatised. Why else would someone opt for a mauve mullet?

SALLY. We should get on. Diane needs the stage back at three.

CHRISTIAN. Okay. Can I get you to stand in your couples? Your ABBA couples, that is. Now, look lovingly at each other. That's beautiful.

They do so. JODIE *and* PETER *just about manage this;*
MRS CAMPBELL *looks a little smitten with* EDWARD.

EDWARD. How's the beard, Mrs C? Still itchy?

MRS CAMPBELL. Yes, dear. A little.

EDWARD. Of course, it's ironic really. Peter has far more
experience with beards than I do.

PETER. Will you pack it in?

CHRISTIAN. Right. Now turn to the camera and smoulder.
Give me sex.

MRS CAMPBELL. I beg your pardon?

CHRISTIAN. Come on, Mrs C. Think of Mr Campbell!

MRS CAMPBELL. That doesn't help.

JODIE. Is there a Mr Campbell?

MRS CAMPBELL. There is. He's in Kirkcaldy and as far as
I'm concerned, he can stay there.

CHRISTIAN *clicks away.*

SALLY. We don't want it too raunchy, do we? That doesn't feel
very… ABBA…

CHRISTIAN *crosses to his bag.*

CHRISTIAN. You'd be surprised. They could be quite
adventurous. They once did a photoshoot naked apart from…
a roll of tinfoil!

*He produces a roll of tinfoil from his bag. He aims his
camera at their shocked expressions.*

SALLY. You're not suggesting –

CHRISTIAN. Everybody say 'Chiquitita'!

A flash. Then a blackout.

Transition: 'Chiquitita' by ABBA.

Scene Three: The Stage

September 2015 – half an hour later.

CHRISTIAN *is packing away his camera equipment.* PETER *sits watching, still in costume and make-up, but no longer wearing his wig.*

PETER. Are you sure I can't help at all?

CHRISTIAN. I'm all done, but thanks.

PETER. Thank *you* for all the support. Your Facebook review was very… forgiving.

CHRISTIAN. Oh, I didn't think you were on Facebook.

PETER. I've finally succumbed.

CHRISTIAN. Great! I'll give you a poke…

PETER. I'll – look forward to it.

CHRISTIAN. Were you any happier with your second gig?

PETER. It was okay. Not the most glamorous venue. A pub in Acock's Green.

CHRISTIAN. A where?

PETER. Acock's Green. It's an actual place.

CHRISTIAN. If you say so.

PETER. We got through it, at least. We had to get changed in the gents'. Edward and I got some very funny looks.

CHRISTIAN. Mmm. Not very showbiz. What next?

PETER. Another pub gig. And a gay couple who saw us perform here want to book us for their wedding reception.

CHRISTIAN. Cool.

PETER. Then if that all goes okay, who knows? As we get nearer Christmas, it'd be nice to get some party bookings.

CHRISTIAN. Ah! Talking of parties, I wanted to put a proposal to you.

PETER. I'm listening.

CHRISTIAN. Well, it's my twenty-fifth birthday in March. I've booked a hotel and I'd love to have you.

A beat.

Head Over Heels, I mean. As the entertainment. For the party.

PETER. Right. Yes, of course. But are you sure? That's a long way off.

CHRISTIAN. Be here before we know it.

PETER. Up in Sheffield?

CHRISTIAN. Yeah. I'd get rooms for you all – as well as the fee. I don't expect a freebie.

PETER. Oh, I'm sure we could do 'mates' rates'.

CHRISTIAN. And if you wanted to stay up there for a few days, I could maybe help you get some other bookings. Widen your circle.

PETER. Sounds good. I'll speak to the others. See what they think.

CHRISTIAN. Of course. Wow. You guys are really living the dream, aren't you?

PETER. Hardly that.

CHRISTIAN. No, I mean it. Literally. D'you know, I have this recurring dream that ABBA have reformed and I'm one of their backing singers? And here you guys are: actually doing it. Standing on that stage, singing ABBA.

PETER. I'm always dreaming that I meet them.

CHRISTIAN. And what are they like?

PETER. They're nice. (*A beat.*) What would you say to them if you met them?

CHRISTIAN. I'd beg them to finally release the full version of 'Just Like That'.

PETER. The Holy Grail! They never will you know.

CHRISTIAN. Yeah, I know… How about you?

PETER. I'd ask them what the backing vocals are in the middle of the chorus of 'One of Us'.

CHRISTIAN. 'One of us is aching, with a heart that's breaking'?

PETER. You see, I think it's 'shaking' not 'aching'.

CHRISTIAN (*weighing this up*). You could be right…

PETER. It'd be nice to know for definite. So, what was it that first got you into them?

CHRISTIAN. I was five years old. My kindergarten teacher taught us 'Thank You for the Music'.

PETER. She had great taste. I got it from my mom. She really loved them. Bought all the records from Macro. She even went to see them live at Bingley Hall in 1979 – that was just before she got ill. My earliest memory is Mom taking me to see *ABBA: The Movie*.

CHRISTIAN. Really?

PETER. I cried because I didn't want it to end.

CHRISTIAN. That's moderately adorable. Oh God, I think I put my foot in it earlier. I thought you and Eddie were an item.

PETER. Really? Oh, by the way, he doesn't like [being called Eddie] –

CHRISTIAN. I think I automatically assumed that any ABBA group must consist of two romantically attached couples!

PETER. Don't worry. You're not the first to think that. Half our school thought we were together.

CHRISTIAN. And did you never go there?

PETER. Never. We just don't think of each other that way.

CHRISTIAN. Well, that's a relief…

PETER. Pardon?

CHRISTIAN (*suddenly embarrassed*). Nothing. Thinking aloud. Well, I'm done. I'd better get my train.

CHRISTIAN goes in to give PETER a hug. Then he lets him go.

I'll email you the best shots and I'll be in touch about the party.

PETER. Yeah. Great. Come down and see the new show. It'll be an improvement, I promise.

CHRISTIAN. You bet!

CHRISTIAN exits. PETER looks thoughtful.

PETER (*rolling his eyes*). One of us is *aching*!

Transition: 'One of Us' by ABBA.

Scene Four: Hotel Suite

December 2015.

JODIE *and* EDWARD *enter. They are bundled up in coats and scarves.* JODIE *is wearing a Santa hat. They are carrying suit-bags, keyboards, guitar, make-up boxes: all the paraphernalia for the show.*

JODIE. Is that everything?

EDWARD. Think so. I still think lugging all this crap around is really stage management's responsibility.

JODIE (*smiling*). And are *you* going to tell Sally that?

EDWARD. You just wait. One of these days – I definitely will.

They remove their coats and scarves. As they do so, JODIE *fetches a small gift-wrapped box from her pocket. She hands it to* EDWARD.

JODIE. It's late and it's not much, but, well, I wanted to say thank you.

EDWARD *unwraps the box. It's a tiny crocheted doll of Frida.*

All my own work.

EDWARD. I'm very touched. Thank you, Julie.

JODIE. It's Jod– !

She notices EDWARD*'s wry smile.*

Oh, you! (*She swipes at him playfully.*) I am going to pay you back. As soon as I can.

EDWARD. Entirely up to you.

JODIE. I want to.

EDWARD. I know you do. But I warn you I'll only go and spend it on something frivolous like a life-size sculpture of Tom Daley, or something pretentious like *The Complete Works of Claus-Steffen Mahnkopf.*

JODIE. The who?

EDWARD. No, that's Roger Daltrey.

JODIE. Well, thank you. It's saved my bacon. Or at least it would. If I ate bacon. Which I don't.

EDWARD. Not another word, or I'll hide your platforms.

They look around the room.

JODIE. Swanky, isn't it?

EDWARD. We've certainly got changed in worse.

JODIE. You'd think they could have given us two rooms though, wouldn't you?

EDWARD. Time of year, I suppose.

JODIE. Will it be a problem that all four of us are in here together?

EDWARD. I can assure you, you'll be perfectly safe.

JODIE. I *know* that. I'm thinking of Mrs Campbell.

EDWARD. You have a point. I've seen her undressing me with her eyes.

JODIE. I meant for *her* privacy, not – Does she really – ?

EDWARD. I suspect hidden lusts burn beneath that tartan exterior.

JODIE. Gosh. Have you seen her yet?

EDWARD. No. Why?

JODIE. She doesn't look well. The poor thing's exhausted. This schedule's been really tough.

EDWARD. Tell me about it. Melvyn's starting to forget how gorgeous I am.

JODIE. Well, we just have to get through tonight, then we can all have a bit of a rest.

MRS CAMPBELL *shuffles in. She's holding a hanky to her nose. She looks terrible.*

Come on, Mrs C, sit down.

JODIE *guides her to a chair.*

Would you like a drink?

EDWARD (*offering his hip flask*). Nip of brandy?

MRS CAMPBELL. I'm okay, thank you, Edward. I just need a wee rest.

JODIE *beckons* EDWARD *into the corner.*

JODIE. She can't do the show like this. She's burning up.

EDWARD. What can we do? We can't cancel. There are a hundred and fifty people in that ballroom.

JODIE. Can we do it without her?

EDWARD. It'll look a bit shit, won't it? Going on as a trio.

MRS CAMPBELL. Edward! I forgot to thank you. For my Christmas box.

EDWARD. Oh, it was nothing.

MRS CAMPBELL. You really shouldn't have. It's very naughty of you to be so profligate!

MRS CAMPBELL *sneezes loudly.*

JODIE. What did you get her?

EDWARD. A new calendar.

SALLY *enters.*

SALLY. Stage all looks fine. They're ready for us to sound-check whenever. Peter's just talking to the manager. They've put his nan on the same table with Melvyn and Diane, so that's nice. (*She clocks their expressions.*) What's the matter?

JODIE. It's Mrs C. She's got a fever.

SALLY. How are you feeling, Hermione? You don't look too clever.

MRS CAMPBELL. I can't shake this cold, that's all. I'm alright, really. (*She sneezes.*)

SALLY. I think we should send you home.

MRS CAMPBELL. But what about the show? It's Hogmanay!

SALLY. Your health is more important. We'll manage.

JODIE. Come on, Mrs C. Let's get you tucked up in bed.

MRS CAMPBELL. Maybe you're right. I'm so sorry. And it looked like it was going to be such fun.

JODIE *helps* MRS CAMPBELL *up and they exit.*

EDWARD. You know what this means, don't you?

SALLY. What?

EDWARD. Only one thing for it. You'll have to do it.

SALLY. What? No. You're kidding. No way.

EDWARD. We don't have any other choice. It's either that or cancel.

SALLY. I can't –

EDWARD. How many times have you watched the show now? You'll probably get more of it right than Mrs Campbell has ever managed.

SALLY. But I'm operating. I can't be in it as well.

EDWARD. You can have your little laptop on a table next to the keyboards.

SALLY. Are you not overlooking one little problem?

SALLY *points to her face.*

EDWARD. Oh, now that's just desperate. It's not like the rest of us are doppelgängers.

SALLY. Do you really think the Kidderminster Metropole can cope with a black Benny?

EDWARD. They were going to have to cope with a slightly dazed Scottish one wearing bifocals!

SALLY. But – but –

EDWARD. No more excuses. You're not exactly my *ideal* husband – and I'm sure I'm not your ideal wife – but we can channel that into our performances.

SALLY. What?

EDWARD. We can portray Frida and Benny in their 'we've only just got married and now we're about to get divorced' phase. After all, what was it you used to say? 'A vaguely human shape wearing a beard.' Even you can manage that, can't you?

SALLY. Oh God…

Transition: 'Happy New Year' by ABBA.

Scene Five: Another Hotel Bedroom (in Sheffield)

March 2016.

Darkness.

A knock on the door.

CHRISTIAN (*offstage whisper*). Hey! Are you still awake?

EDWARD. Who is it?

CHRISTIAN (*offstage*). It's the birthday boy. Can I come in?

> EDWARD *sits up in bed and flicks on the bedside lamp. He glances at his phone.*

EDWARD. Bloody hell...

> *He gets out of bed and goes to the door. He opens it.*

Is everything alright?

> CHRISTIAN *enters, carrying a bottle of wine and two glasses. He is a little drunk.*

CHRISTIAN. Everything's wonderful, Eddie. I just didn't want the party to end yet.

EDWARD. You know it's three-thirty in the morning?

CHRISTIAN. Then the night is young. You not going to invite me in? I come bearing refreshments...

EDWARD. Er, I'm not sure –

CHRISTIAN. Come on. It's not like you to turn down a drink.

> *He pours a glass and hands it to* EDWARD. *He does the same for himself.*

Bottoms up!

> *He takes a swig and collapses onto the bed.*

Nice hotel, isn't it?

EDWARD. Yes. Very good of you to put us up here.

CHRISTIAN. I thought we all deserved a treat. And you're only twenty-five once, after all. You know, everyone was raving about the show.

EDWARD. Really?

CHRISTIAN. Of course! They loved you. And Sally's starting to look like she's enjoying it now. A bit.

EDWARD. Yes. She even remembers to smile occasionally. Although rarely in my direction.

CHRISTIAN. Ha! Why don't you come and sit down?

EDWARD *does so hesitantly.*

You're very quiet, Eddie. You're not usually lost for words.

EDWARD. Please don't call me – Oh never mind.

CHRISTIAN. You look nervous. Don't be nervous. I won't bite… I promise.

EDWARD. What are you doing here, Christian?

CHRISTIAN. I told you. All my friends have left. And I'm not ready for the party to end just yet.

CHRISTIAN *holds* EDWARD*'s gaze. They both breathe.*

Eventually CHRISTIAN *reaches over and places his hand on* EDWARD*'s knee. All* EDWARD *can do is look at him helplessly.*

I like you, Eddie. I like you a lot.

EDWARD. Well I like you, but I thought… Well, you've been spending a lot of time with Peter.

CHRISTIAN. Peter's a friend. That's all. We talk about ABBA together. With you, I want to do … other stuff.

EDWARD. What kind of… other stuff?

CHRISTIAN *places a finger on* EDWARD*'s lips.*

CHRISTIAN. Hush now. And let me show you.

CHRISTIAN *traces his finger around* EDWARD's *mouth.*
Then he leans in to kiss him. EDWARD's *body stiffens for*
a moment. And then he surrenders and kisses him back.
The two of them fall into the bed.

Transition: 'Like an Angel Passing Through My Room' by
ABBA.

Scene Six: The Back Room of a Pub

June 2016.

PETER *is sitting at a table. There is a laptop in front of him.*
He is partially dressed in Agnetha's Eurovision costume,
although he is wearing his dressing gown and his long, blonde
wig covers his face. His shoulders are shaking and he is
sobbing uncontrollably.

SALLY *enters. Alarmed, she rushes to* PETER's *side. She gets*
a hanky and tries to wipe his face.

SALLY. Peter! Peter! Oh, what is it, baby? What's the matter?

PETER *shakes his head, unable to speak.*

Oh God, what's happened? Is it – is it your nan?

PETER *shakes his head again.*

Thank God for that. Come on, now. Calm down. Breathe.
That's it. Breathe. Nice and deep.

PETER *slowly starts to recover his composure.*

Look at you. You've made a right mess of your make-up.

He points at the laptop in front of him.

What are you looking at? YouTube?

PETER *nods.*

PETER. It's just been uploaded. Footage. Footage of –

SALLY (*reading off the screen*). Agnetha and Frida sing 'The Way Old Friends Do'. Berns Restaurant. Stockholm. June 2016.

PETER. There was a party last week. Celebrating fifty years since Benny and Björn met. Some of their friends sang. And one of the guests – filmed it on his phone…

SALLY. And this is why you're crying??

PETER. Never in my life did I think I'd hear them sing together again… And there's a moment when Frida puts her arm around… Oh it just finished me off…

SALLY. Bloody hell, Peter. You frightened me to death! I thought – Well, God knows what I thought. I heard you sobbing from the bar.

PETER. I'm sorry. It's just a bit… overwhelming.

SALLY *starts to laugh in spite of herself.*

SALLY. You're a bloody idiot.

PETER (*sheepishly*). I'm sorry.

SALLY *gives him a hug.*

SALLY. It's okay. You're my bloody idiot.

She strokes his hair.

You alright now?

PETER. Yeah. I'm fine.

SALLY. Good. Cos I did actually want to talk to you. Though I'm not sure you're in a fit state for any more shocks.

PETER. That sounds ominous, but go ahead. I can cope.

SALLY. It's Diane.

PETER. Go on.

SALLY. She needs me, Peter.

PETER. The IVF?

> SALLY *shakes her head.*

> Oh, I'm so sorry, Sal.

SALLY. We knew all along it was only a slim chance. At our age.

PETER. So what next?

SALLY. Well, all this. Head Over Heels was only meant to be a one-off, right? And now here we are: a whole year on. Diane has been so patient –

PETER. But she needs you. I get that. Of course I do.

SALLY. We barely see each other. So I've decided, I'll do all the bookings we have in the diary, but then I'm going to call it a day.

PETER. I understand. Completely.

SALLY. Great. So, this – (*She gestures to the laptop.*) you break your heart over. But when your best mate quits your band, it's a shrug and a 'meh'.

> *She grins at him. He smiles in return.*

PETER (*pulling on his platform boots*). To be honest, I'm amazed you ever agreed to do it in the first place.

SALLY. Well you have Edward to thank for that.

PETER. He does have some uses, then.

> SALLY *smiles.*

SALLY. Good old Benny. I'll miss him. You know, Diane kind of fancies me in the beard. I might nick it.

PETER. You be careful. That thing's like velcro. If the two of you got carried away, you could end up giving her a Brazilian.

SALLY. I'll bear that in mind!

PETER. Do you think we could persuade Mrs C to come back?

SALLY. I doubt it. She's making the most of having her evenings again – and I'm not really sure you can compete with *Gareth*.

PETER. Gareth?

SALLY. The big, burly bloke who painted her window frames last summer. By all accounts, her patio doors are not the only things he's been touching up...

PETER. Good for her. I'll have to advertise then. And we could do with some standbys to learn the show as well. I mean: what if one of us gets ill again?

SALLY. I'd always step in if you were desperate.

PETER. Thanks, love. But there is another reason...

SALLY. Ah. The elephant in the room.

PETER. I mean, he's always liked a drink, I know that, but these last few months...

SALLY. I could smell it on him at the Redditch gig. I wondered if you'd noticed.

PETER. I'm sure everyone did – from the bus station all the way to the Kingfisher Centre! Oh, he does a pretty good job of hiding it, but it's definitely getting worse.

SALLY. Have you talked to him at all?

PETER. I've tried. He says he's not drinking any more than usual, and besides, he can handle it. I ask him if anything's wrong and he says no.

SALLY. Maybe being apart is causing problems for him and Melvyn too.

PETER. He says not but what can I do if he won't talk to me?

SALLY. Not a lot.

PETER. I couldn't have done this without you, you know.

SALLY. I know.

PETER. Who's going to deal with all those pub landlords now?

SALLY. You'll just have to find yourself another Rottweiler!
Speaking of landlords, I'd better go collect our fee.

She heads to the door.

PETER. If you see her 'Serene Highness' in there, tell him to
get a shift on, will you?

Transition: 'Move On' by ABBA.

Scene Seven: Spa Terrace

August 2016.

EDWARD, *in a white fluffy dressing gown and slippers, is
sitting reading* The Observer. *A glass of wine sits beside him.*

CHRISTIAN *enters, sneaks up behind him and kisses him on
the neck.*

CHRISTIAN. What ya reading about?

EDWARD *reaches up to touch* CHRISTIAN*'s face.*

EDWARD. Hate crime. It's rocketed since the referendum.

CHRISTIAN. Ah well. I reckon we'll be okay. Theresa will get
it all sorted.

EDWARD. *Theresa?* Oh, don't tell me you're a Tory.

CHRISTIAN. No, I'm not a Tory. I just think she looks like she
knows what she's doing.

EDWARD. *Jesus...*

CHRISTIAN. And she's an ABBA fan! 'Dancing Queen' was
one of her Desert Island Discs.

EDWARD. Christian, you cannot assess a person's integrity and
ability simply by whether or not they like ABBA! Oh God,

let's not talk politics. It's too depressing. I've been looking
forward to this weekend for too long.

EDWARD *kisses* CHRISTIAN.

CHRISTIAN. What did you tell Melvyn in the end?

EDWARD. That I've taken Mother to a spa for her birthday.

CHRISTIAN. Isn't that a bit risky? What if they speak?

EDWARD. Mother and Melvyn haven't spoken in twenty years.
I think we're safe.

CHRISTIAN. I guess that is lucky.

EDWARD *kisses him again and starts to unbutton his shirt.*

EDWARD. Now take your clothes off and let me see that
true-blue arse of yours…

CHRISTIAN *pulls away a little.*

I'm only joking. I don't really think you're a Tory.

CHRISTIAN. I know. I'm sorry. I'm just a bit out of sorts.

EDWARD. Why? Talk to me.

CHRISTIAN. It's nothing. Oh, did Peter tell you I've found us
a new Benny?

EDWARD. Have you?

CHRISTIAN. Yeah, I asked my friend Zamira.

EDWARD. Right. No, Peter didn't mention it.

CHRISTIAN. She's dual heritage: half Malaysian, half
Aboriginal, so it keeps the band's diversity, which I think is
important, don't you?

EDWARD. Er, yeah. Definitely.

CHRISTIAN. And she's an amazing pianist, so she could play
live if you wanted her to…

EDWARD. Great.

EDWARD *tries to kiss him again*.

CHRISTIAN. You're not really talking to Peter much nowadays, are you?

EDWARD. Not much. I don't trust myself. In case I let something slip –

CHRISTIAN. I know. I know. And I guess that's the right thing to do.

EDWARD. I'm eaten up with guilt about all of this as it is. I don't want to put Peter in that position: having to lie to Melvyn to cover up for me.

CHRISTIAN. I understand. I do.

EDWARD *tops up his wine glass*.

Of course, you could do something to put an end to all the guilt.

EDWARD. Uh-uh. The guilt never ends. Holy Mother Mary saw to that many years ago.

CHRISTIAN. Well, maybe not the guilt. But the secrecy. And the lies.

EDWARD. What are you getting at?

CHRISTIAN. You could tell Melvyn. About us.

EDWARD. Are you being serious?

CHRISTIAN. Eddie, I'm sick of illicit phone calls and looking over our shoulders in case anyone recognises us when we're out together. I don't want to share you any more. And I want to tell the whole world about the man I love.

EDWARD. Love?

CHRISTIAN. Yes, Edward. I love you. Otherwise, what do you think this is?

EDWARD. I don't know. A diversion? A drunken fumble that's somehow managed to last all these months? I'm a confused, middle-aged man having a textbook midlife crisis. You're in the prime of your life. And you're gorgeous.

CHRISTIAN. And I want to be with you.

EDWARD. Can't you see what you're asking me to do?
Melvyn – he's the only life I've ever known. I can't do that
to him. It would destroy him.

CHRISTIAN. But why should you have to compromise? You
have the rest of your life ahead of you. And you deserve to
be happy. You're kind and generous and funny and sexy...

EDWARD. Do you really mean all that?

CHRISTIAN. Of course I do! Look, how many times do I have
to say it to convince you? I'm into older guys. Always have
been. I thought you might understand that better than most.

EDWARD. Well, yes, but – but what would we do? Where
would we go?

CHRISTIAN. We can get a place together. We could even go
back to Sydney if you like. As long as we're together.

He cradles EDWARD*'s face tenderly and kisses him.*

Please, darling. I love you.

EDWARD. I love you too.

Transition: 'I've Been Waiting for You' by ABBA.

Scene Eight: Shirley Golf Club

August 2016.

JODIE *– dressed in her Björn costume – is on her mobile.*
She paces up and down. Hangs up. Dials again.

PETER *enters, wearing Agnetha's blue cat dress costume.*

PETER. Any joy?

JODIE. It just keeps going to voicemail.

PETER. Bloody hell. What are we gonna do?

JODIE. Zamira said she could play a few instrumentals. Fill
time and hope he gets here.

PETER. And if he doesn't turn up? Shirley Golf Club have
booked an ABBA tribute band. They're not going to pay if
we're missing an 'A'.

JODIE. Hey, that rhymed! (*A beat.*) Sorry.

CHRISTIAN *enters.*

CHRISTIAN. Hi, guys! Everything okay?

JODIE. Oh hi. I didn't know you were coming today.

CHRISTIAN. Yeah, I'm gonna take some new shots of you all –
now Zamira's up and running.

PETER. God, yes. Sorry. I forgot. We're in a bit of a crisis.

CHRISTIAN. Really?

PETER. Edward's gone AWOL. He's not answering his phone.
His mom doesn't know where he is.

CHRISTIAN. Have you tried Melvyn?

JODIE. He's not picking up either. Oh, I hope nothing's
happened.

PETER. He's probably asleep – or hungover. I *knew* this was
going to happen one day.

CHRISTIAN. What are you gonna do?

PETER. Zamira's buying us some time. If he's not here in five minutes, we either offer them a Frida-free show, or we cancel. I should have got my arse in gear and put those adverts in *The Stage*...

A beat. The three of them contemplate this.

CHRISTIAN. Or I do it.

PETER. What?

CHRISTIAN. I've seen the show so many times now. And I know all the songs after all.

PETER. Would you? Could you?

CHRISTIAN. Are you kidding? It'd be an honour.

JODIE. What have we got to lose, Peter?

Sudden activity. PETER *fetches the Frida costume from the rail.*

PETER. Will the costume fit?

CHRISTIAN *takes his shirt off.*

CHRISTIAN. Only one way to find out.

JODIE. I'll tell Zamira.

PETER. Oh, can you tell Bruce, as well? He should be in the office.

JODIE. Is he the one with the elbows?

PETER. Er – yes?

She nods and exits.

CHRISTIAN *continues to strip off as* PETER *fetches a pair of tights from a large canvas bag. He starts to roll up one leg and gestures to a chair.*

Sit down. There's a knack to this.

CHRISTIAN *sits and offers his foot.*

CHRISTIAN. Good job I booked that pedicure!

PETER *starts to dress him.* CHRISTIAN *reaches down to help.*

PETER. Careful! You'll ladder them.

CHRISTIAN. Sorry! It's my first time in pantyhose!

PETER. Don't worry about harmonies. If you're not sure, just stick to the tune.

CHRISTIAN. Peter, it's me you're talking to. I know the harmonies.

PETER. Of course. Sorry. What do you want to do about the dance solo in 'Gimme'?

CHRISTIAN. I might sit that one out. Is that okay?

PETER. Yes, of course.

CHRISTIAN. I've always thought it was a bit tacky anyway…

PETER *measures the bra against* CHRISTIAN*'s chest.*

PETER. We'll have to lose the bra. You're too broad.

CHRISTIAN. I'll just have to be a 'Flat-chested Frida'.

PETER. Seems a bit unfair when I have a padded bottom…

CHRISTIAN (*sleazy, Australian journalist impression*). 'Agg-nee-thuh – I read somewhere that you are the proud owner of an award, which declares you as the lady with the most sexiest bottom in Europe. Is that true?'

PETER (*Agnetha impression*). 'How can I answer to that? I haven't seen it.'

They laugh as CHRISTIAN *starts to pull on his platform boots.*

Oh you can't wear those!

CHRISTIAN. What's wrong with them?

PETER. How tall are you?

CHRISTIAN. Six-two.

PETER. Those are five-inch platforms. You'll look like Frankenstein's monster next to me.

CHRISTIAN. Well that's charming!

PETER. Oh, you know I didn't mean it like that!

CHRISTIAN. I could wear my trainers. They have a more modest heel.

PETER. I think that would be for the best.

CHRISTIAN puts his trainers back on. PETER watches in bewilderment.

This is so crazy.

PETER holds out Frida's yellow cat dress and CHRISTIAN pulls it on.

It's a bit tight on you.

CHRISTIAN. It's okay.

CHRISTIAN does a twirl.

How do I look?

PETER. Like an angel passing through my room! Now, we don't have time to do full make-up. We'll have to settle for some lipstick and a bit of eyeshadow.

CHRISTIAN. Okay.

PETER. You've saved the day, Christian.

CHRISTIAN. Well, you owe me one.

They look at each other, and then they both move in for a long kiss. They pause.

I don't think I've ever been more turned on in my life.

PETER. Maybe we *should* cancel…

They're about to kiss again when JODIE suddenly bursts in. PETER and CHRISTIAN hurriedly move apart.

JODIE. It's okay! Panic over. He's here, he's here.

EDWARD *enters. He's clearly very drunk.*

EDWARD. Yes, panic over. I'm here. I'm here. Where's Shakira?

JODIE. Zamira.

EDWARD. Whatever.

He sees CHRISTIAN.

What the – ?

PETER. Where have you been? We've been frantic!

EDWARD. Why's he here?

CHRISTIAN. Edward…

EDWARD. Oh *now* you choose to get my name right.

PETER. Can we discuss this later? We're about to do a show and you're clearly in no condition –

EDWARD. Oh yes, the show must go on. My whole life has come crashing down around my ears, but we mustn't let that interfere with the show, must we?

PETER. I think you should leave.

EDWARD (*to* CHRISTIAN). What *are* you?

CHRISTIAN. Please, Edward…

PETER. Don't go turning on Christian. He's helping us out, that's all.

EDWARD. How could you? What have you made me do? I've ruined everything.

He sinks to the floor, his head in his hands. JODIE *crouches beside him.*

JODIE. What's happened?

EDWARD. What's happened? I've told Melvyn it's over, that's what's happened. I've told him I'm in love with someone else.

CHRISTIAN. Oh God.

EDWARD. All this time I've been agonising over it. And then
I finally pluck up the courage – tell my husband I don't love
him any more. And when I call you with the news – (*He looks
at* CHRISTIAN.) you tell me you 'don't feel the same way'.

Silence.

JODIE. I don't understand.

PETER. What are you talking about? (*To* CHRISTIAN.) What's
he talking about?

CHRISTIAN. Oh God. I so hoped it wouldn't come to this.

PETER. Is one of you going to explain?

EDWARD. If I understood, I would.

CHRISTIAN. I'm so sorry, Peter. I thought I could keep this
under control. Manage the situation.

JODIE. Maybe I should go –

CHRISTIAN. Okay. Here goes. At my birthday party, back in
March, Edward made it clear that he'd developed feelings
for me.

EDWARD (*weakly*). What?

CHRISTIAN. I tried to let him down gently. I dunno, maybe
I should have been more forceful, but I thought if I just
didn't engage, he'd get over it and he'd move on.

EDWARD. I – I –

CHRISTIAN. He sent me messages, gifts. He told me he'd
fallen in love with me. And then he said he was going to
leave Melvyn. I said no. I said it was a fantasy, that I just
don't feel that way about him. But Edward said that it would
prove how much he loved me. And then we could finally be
together.

EDWARD. That – that isn't true.

PETER. Oh God.

EDWARD *fumbles for his phone.*

EDWARD. I have text messages. Look – look –

He locates the messages and hands the phone to JODIE.

Read – read them…

JODIE. I don't think I should.

EDWARD. Read!

JODIE. 'I want you so much. Can't wait to spend the whole weekend with you.' 'You're so beautiful. You mean the world to me.' 'I'm going to tell Melvyn. Wish me luck. I love you so.'

EDWARD. See! See!

JODIE (*gently*). But Edward… These are all from you. There are no replies to any of them.

EDWARD. Well, no. We agreed. We said it was too risky. In case Melvyn was with me and saw the texts come in. So Christian said – he said he wouldn't reply.

CHRISTIAN. I'm so sorry about this, Edward. But this is all in your head. You need help.

EDWARD. No, no, no…

PETER. I'm calling you a taxi. You need to go to your mother's and sober up.

JODIE. I'll do it.

JODIE steps aside and makes the call.

EDWARD (*to* PETER). Surely you believe me?

PETER. You know what? I think the scales have finally fallen from my eyes.

EDWARD. What?

PETER. All these years, I've defended you. But I see it now. There's a pattern to this. Barney Bailey. Jonathan Harris. Now Christian. How many more have there been? If someone isn't interested in you, yeah it's tough, but you have to accept it. I mean, I get it: unrequited love is awful, but you can't force people to fall for you. That's deeply fucked up. It really is. You're a mess, Edward. Now you can blame it on your parents, on religion, on the booze. There's always something to blame, isn't there? But Christian's right. You need help. Melvyn's a good man. He loves you. More than you know. And certainly more than you deserve. Maybe he'll forgive you. And maybe one day you'll forgive yourself.

EDWARD *looks at him in despair.*

CHRISTIAN *slowly takes* PETER*'s hand and kisses it. He looks at* EDWARD *with pity.*

EDWARD. You're not… The two of you…?

CHRISTIAN. I'm sorry, Edward. I really am.

EDWARD. How long?

CHRISTIAN. A few weeks. We couldn't fight it any longer, Edward.

PETER. We don't have to explain ourselves, Christian. And we certainly don't have anything to apologise for.

EDWARD. I think I'm going to be sick.

PETER. Well, please don't do it in here.

EDWARD. I want my costume.

PETER. Just. Go.

EDWARD. Give me my costume! I want my fucking cat costume!

PETER. Oh, give it to him. Anything to make him leave.

CHRISTIAN *takes off the dress and hands it to* EDWARD, *who snatches it from him.*

EDWARD. I hope you'll be very happy together. And I guess now you can put 'The Day Before You Came' in the show and the two of you can sing it to your hearts' content.

He exits.

A beat.

JODIE. The cab's on its way. I'll make sure he gets in it.

She exits.

PETER *crumples into* CHRISTIAN*'s arms.*

PETER. Oh God.

CHRISTIAN. Shhh… It's okay. You did the right thing. It's all gonna be okay.

Transition: 'The Day Before You Came' by ABBA.

Scene Nine: Peter's Flat

2 September 2021.

The music fades out.

RADIO DJ (*voice-over*). That was 'The Day Before You Came'. That's one of Malcolm's favourites, you know.

And they always said they'd never do it! Get back together? Never in a million years! But you know what? They've actually gone and done it. And after everything we've all been through this past eighteen months, I reckon the one thing the world really needs right now is the return of ABBA. I mean that. I'm not being sarky for once. So stick with us, and we'll be playing their brand-new song – exclusively for you lot – just a bit later on!

SALLY *bustles out of the kitchen with a tray of cheese and pineapple on sticks. The sticks all have little Swedish flags on them.*

But before we get to that, you've been telling us all about your weirdest celebrity crushes, and I've got a text here from Janice in Milton Keynes. She says she's developed a thing for Dr Chris Whitty. Apparently she's in thrall to his animal magnetism and the way he never blinks when he looks into the camera. And she says whenever she hears 'Next slide, please', she gets a hot flush – and gets a bit moist! Well, Janice, if I were you I'd have a cold shower and, I dunno, watch *Home and Away* –

SALLY *switches off the radio as* MRS CAMPBELL *enters with some napkins.*

MRS CAMPBELL. I wonder if I should have brought the pickled herring.

SALLY. They'd have been a bold choice.

MRS CAMPBELL. I still think Peter would appreciate them.

SALLY. Do you reckon?

MRS CAMPBELL. It would have fitted with the whole theme. ABBA had to negotiate with a canned fish factory to get permission to use the name, you know, way back in 1974. The Abba Seafood Company is still going strong. Their main factory is situated in a place called Kungshamn.

SALLY. How on earth do you – ?

SALLY *stops as* MRS CAMPBELL *beams at her.*

That glossary's really stuck with you, hasn't it?

The doorbell rings.

(*Shouting back into the kitchen.*) I'll get it!

SALLY *opens the front door.*

Oh, we weren't sure whether you could come!

JODIE *enters, followed by* SALLY.

JODIE. Wouldn't have missed it for the world – and we don't have a show tonight, anyway. (*She spots* MRS CAMPBELL.) Mrs C! It's been ages.

MRS CAMPBELL. Hullo!

JODIE. Are we hugging?

MRS CAMPBELL. Of course we are!

They hug.

JODIE. You look so well!

MRS CAMPBELL. Thank you, dear.

JODIE. Am I late?

SALLY. No. I've only been here about half an hour. Hermione got here yesterday.

MRS CAMPBELL. I've not been here since then. I went home when nobody answered the door.

JODIE. Now I need to have a stern word with you, Mrs C. You never reply to my voicenotes.

MRS CAMPBELL. I'm sorry, dear. I just don't trust mobile phones. I worry about the radiation.

JODIE. Where's Peter?

SALLY. In the kitchen. He's pretty nervous. For multiple reasons.

JODIE. I can imagine. You don't think he'll actually show up, do you?

SALLY. Unlikely, I'd have thought.

MRS CAMPBELL. Have you stayed in touch with him?

JODIE. We're Facebook friends, but he never posts anything. And after what happened, it all feels a bit – awkward...

JODIE crosses to the shelf and picks up a framed photo. It's a promotional shot of the original line-up of Head Over Heels.

Did Peter put this here?

SALLY. No. I found it in a drawer. Thought I'd risk it.

JODIE. Right.

PETER enters.

PETER. Oh, I'm so glad you could make it.

JODIE. Me too. (*Spreading her arms.*) Are we – [hugging]?

PETER *laughs and embraces her.*

It's finally the big day then! How are you feeling?

PETER. I've been in a state of extreme nervous anticipation for several hours now. I never dreamt that –

The doorbell rings. They all look at each other.

JODIE. Ah…

SALLY (*to* PETER). You okay?

PETER. I hear the doorbell ring and suddenly the panic takes me…

He takes a deep breath, goes to the door and opens it.

I didn't think you'd come.

EDWARD *enters.*

EDWARD. I very nearly didn't.

PETER. Come in. The gang's all here.

PETER *steps to one side.*

EDWARD. Gosh. Hello… Head Over Heels.

JODIE *comes up to hug* EDWARD. EDWARD *steps back.*

I'm not – (*By way of explanation.*) Melvyn…

An awkward pause.

SALLY. Can I get you a drink?

EDWARD. Not any more, you'll all be relieved to hear.

SALLY. Soft drink?

EDWARD. Water would be lovely. Thank you.

SALLY *exits to the kitchen.* EDWARD *spots and picks up the framed picture.*

PETER. Good times, eh?

EDWARD. For the most part. How is Sally?

PETER. She's well. Busy. She and Diane have become foster parents.

EDWARD. Poor kids won't know what's hit them.

SALLY re-enters with the water and gives it to EDWARD.

SALLY. I heard that.

EDWARD. How about you, Mrs C? Any pattering of tiny feet coming from your direction?

MRS CAMPBELL. Get away with you, Edward. I am courting though: a strapping fellow named Steve.

PETER. He's a carpet fitter from Moseley Village.

MRS CAMPBELL. He has tattoos in places I never even knew you *could* tattoo.

EDWARD. I'm delighted to hear it. I always knew you were a dark horse.

MRS CAMPBELL. I'm 'living my best life'. Isn't that what the young people say nowadays?

EDWARD (*to* JODIE). How's work?

JODIE. Oh, you know, not bad. I'm touring. With the *Peppa Pig Live Show*. I'm giving my 'Madame Gazelle'.

EDWARD. You finally landed a female role. Congratulations.

JODIE. Well, she's a female *gazelle*. But thank you.

A beat.

SALLY. Should we – leave you two to talk for a bit?

PETER. No, I think I'd like all of you to hear this. If that's alright with you. (*He gathers himself.*) Edward, I owe you an apology.

EDWARD. Yes, you said that in your message.

PETER. This is my apology. I'm sorry. I should have believed you.

EDWARD *takes this in*.

EDWARD. So what happened?

PETER. It pretty much all went to shit, that's what happened.

EDWARD. Quelle surprise…

PETER. Not straight away. He – Christian – joined the band.
Took your place. Things were okay for a while. I thought we
were happy. I even introduced him to my nan.

EDWARD. That must have been – Oh, your nan – is she…?

PETER. She's still going strong.

EDWARD. Good. Carry on.

PETER. Well, before long, things started to feel – off. With the
band and with him and me.

PETER *trails off and* JODIE *picks up the tale*.

JODIE. Zamira kept banging on about playing live: she thought it
was a waste of her talents *pretending* to do something she
could actually do for real. And of course, I couldn't play the
guitar. Then I came across some pretty horrible posts about me
on ABBA Chat – you know, the Facebook group? I mean, I
don't know that they were anything to do with Christian, but,
well, in any case, it knocked my confidence. It just didn't feel
like fun any more.

PETER. And when Jodie left, Christian had another brilliant
suggestion for a replacement. We carried on for a few more
months, but it wasn't the same. I felt like an outsider. And
Christian was starting to become… distant. The plan was
he'd move in here but somehow it never seemed to be the
right time. So when he very gently suggested that I didn't
quite fit in with the band any more, it was hard to disagree.
Agnetha was supposed to be the baby of the group – and
there was me, old enough to be their father.

EDWARD. So you just gave up? Walked away and handed it all
over to him?

PETER. He bought the costumes off me, changed the name.

MRS CAMPBELL. They're called ABBA-Dabba-Do now.

EDWARD. Was that when you realised I'd been telling the truth?

PETER. I guess it dawned on me gradually. I didn't want to admit it. I'd been so blinded by Christian, and his charm and his beauty, I couldn't think straight.

EDWARD. Yes, he has that effect on people. Do you think he's a sociopath? Surely he didn't go to all that trouble just to take over our stupid band?

SALLY. I can't believe he had it planned all along.

JODIE. That would be pretty – psychotic, wouldn't it?

PETER. I reckon he just got off on the power trip.

EDWARD. You mean wrapping two silly old fools round his little finger?

PETER. Yeah. Then, once the chase was over, he got bored, I guess.

EDWARD. And as collateral, he got to turn his dream into reality. He's finally singing with ABBA. Well, with ABBA-Dabba-Do.

SALLY. Diane has promised she'll never book them to perform at the Library Theatre.

EDWARD. In that case, we're all square and I no longer bear him any ill-will.

JODIE. Really?

EDWARD. No. Of course not. I hope someone with antibiotic-resistant gonorrhoea comes in his eye. Both eyes. Sorry, Mrs C. That was a bit – graphic.

MRS CAMPBELL. No, I think that sounds quite fair. Under the circumstances.

PETER. So, Melvyn took you back?

EDWARD *turns to* JODIE, SALLY *and* MRS CAMPBELL.

EDWARD. I don't want to be all 'can the ladies retire to the kitchen'? But is there a smorgasbord desperately crying out for your combined attention?

SALLY. Come on, you two. Let's fetch the lingonberries.

SALLY, JODIE and MRS CAMPBELL exit to the kitchen.

EDWARD. You said a lot of hurtful things to me in that golf club, Peter. But most – maybe all of it – happened to be true. Certainly what you said about Melvyn. We've worked through a lot of stuff these past few years. He's a good man. A very good man. And he's more than I deserve.

PETER. Don't put yourself down.

EDWARD. Why? Because that's *your* speciality?

PETER smiles.

PETER. I abandoned you when you needed me. Again. I've been a pretty shit friend, all things considered.

EDWARD. I didn't exactly make it easy. I'm hardly Sir Galahad.

PETER. Well, that's true.

EDWARD. So, this evening. What made you get in touch? After all this time?

PETER takes a deep breath and then sings.

PETER.
'You and I can share the silence.
Finding comfort together.
The way old friends do…'

He pauses. He looks at EDWARD hopefully. After a moment, EDWARD sighs.

EDWARD. This is so cheesy. I can't believe I'm doing this…

He sings.

'And after fights and words of violence.
We make up with each other.
The way old friends do.'

They sing together in harmony.

PETER/EDWARD.
    'Times of joy and times of sorrow.
    We will always see it through.

PETER. Oh…

PETER/EDWARD.
    I don't care what comes tomorrow.
    We can face it together.
    The way old friends do…'

EDWARD. It hasn't ruined it for you then? What happened with Head Over Heels. You still listen to the music?

PETER. ABBA have got me through so much. I listen to them when I'm on top of the world; I listen to them when I'm at my lowest ebb. Those four Swedes – well, three Swedes and a Norwegian – they'll never know how much joy they've given me. Their music always manages to make me feel my mom isn't so far away. And I'm not going to let some twat with big blue eyes and an arse you could bury your face in for days fuck that up.

EDWARD. Good for you.

PETER. Although, admittedly, I no longer patronise the ABBA Chat Facebook group.

EDWARD. You never trusted Facebook, anyway.

The alarm on PETER*'s mobile goes off.*

PETER. Oh God. There we go. It's time. (*Calling to the kitchen.*) Sally! Jodie! Mrs C!

EDWARD. Are you ready for this?

PETER. Ready as I'll ever be.

EDWARD. You were always adamant they'd never actually get back together.

PETER. Yep. Something else I got completely wrong.

EDWARD. I'm glad you called.

PETER. I'm glad you came. There's nobody else I'd rather have with me when I hear this music for the first time.

EDWARD *glances around, spots the box of tissues on the shelf and brings it over to* PETER.

Thanks.

EDWARD. What's the new song called again?

PETER. 'I Still Have Faith in You'.

They smile.

PETER *turns the radio on.*

Transition: 'I Still Have Faith in You' by ABBA.

Curtain Call

Lights up on:

MRS CAMPBELL – *dressed as Benny – standing at the keyboard. The introduction to 'Dancing Queen' kicks in. She steps forward, takes her bow and then returns behind the keyboard.*

JODIE – *dressed as Björn – enters. She takes her bow.*

CHRISTIAN – *dressed as Frida – enters. He is wearing the accursed purple spiky wig. He takes his bow.*

SALLY – *also dressed as Benny – enters. She taps* CHRISTIAN *on the shoulder and sends him to stand upstage. She takes her bow and then stands beside* MRS CAMPBELL *behind the keyboard.*

Finally, PETER *and* EDWARD – *dressed as Agnetha and Frida – enter.*

They take their bow.

End.

www.nickhernbooks.co.uk

facebook.com/nickhernbooks

twitter.com/nickhernbooks